THE DEPLORABLE WORD

Constantine Charagma

&

Erica Frevel

THE DEPLORABLE WORD

THE DEPLORABLE WORD
VOLUME 1

© 2016 Constantine Charagma and Erica Frevel

ISBN-13: 978-0997836318
ISBN-10: 0997836318

COVER ART by ERICA FREVEL
EDITED by RIKKI K

YID CHES MUN NAG LAM SET AN

DISCLAIMER:
All material contained in this document is provided for research and educational purposes only. *Caveat lector.*

THE DEPLORABLE WORD

SACRED ART

Each collage in this book is an altarpiece with sigils hidden throughout. These sigils will activate with proper use. If there is a particular collage that you can't seem to look away from, that is the piece you should begin with. The collages that represent Satan, Choronzon and Lillith in this book are used together as a triptych altarpiece. If you came to the worship of the Abyss through any of these Entities, Satan in my case, those altarpieces will be most effective for you.

Be warned that successfully activating the entire collection within this book may result in a dangerous amount of Void energy in the area. It is very possible that this energy will mark you as an enemy of the natural world... be prepared for hostilities.

Use a sharp knife (preferably a ritual blade) to cut the altarpiece out of the book. In order to activate the inherent power in each one you must add blood to the area of the collage that first pulls your eye toward it. Whatever that location, it is the center point of the gateway which will allow you to open your altar up to the frequency of the Void. Use your own blood or that of a sacrifice using the process of bloodletting discussed in this book.

Arrange the altarpiece on an established altar and anoint with the fumes of burnt offerings of hair, skin, nails and incense combined. Light candles or keep a fire burning, but be sure to have complete darkness otherwise. Seated in meditation position, soften the gaze on the altarpiece and begin to call forth the great darkness. These calls are not vocal calls, but a beacon of shadow in the light of the cosmos. Call from a place deep in the gut and from the back of the skull as these are the most primal parts of the human anatomy. When you begin to feel a harsh vibration or sharp sensations, intensify your gaze and stare directly at the area in which you have applied the blood. Invite the fear inside your gut and mind. Violent shifts in consciousness are to be expected as well as backlash from the natural order around you. Once you feel the undeniable presence of the ancient dark, your work is done and the energy cannot be made to leave. Attempting to reverse this activation is not possible and will only worsen the effects on your end.

Keep the altarpieces out of direct sunlight. Reactivate if the gateway begins to close.

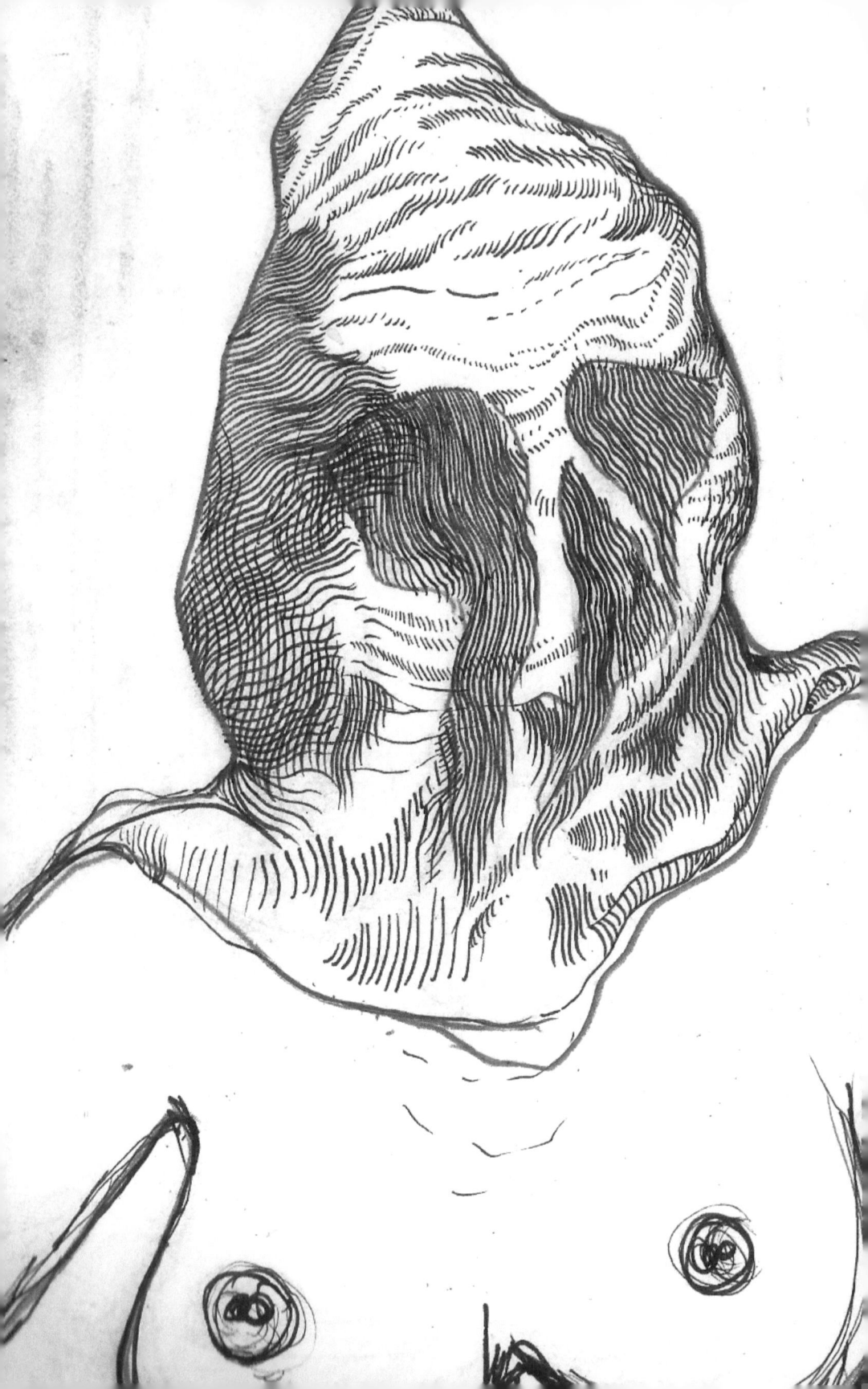

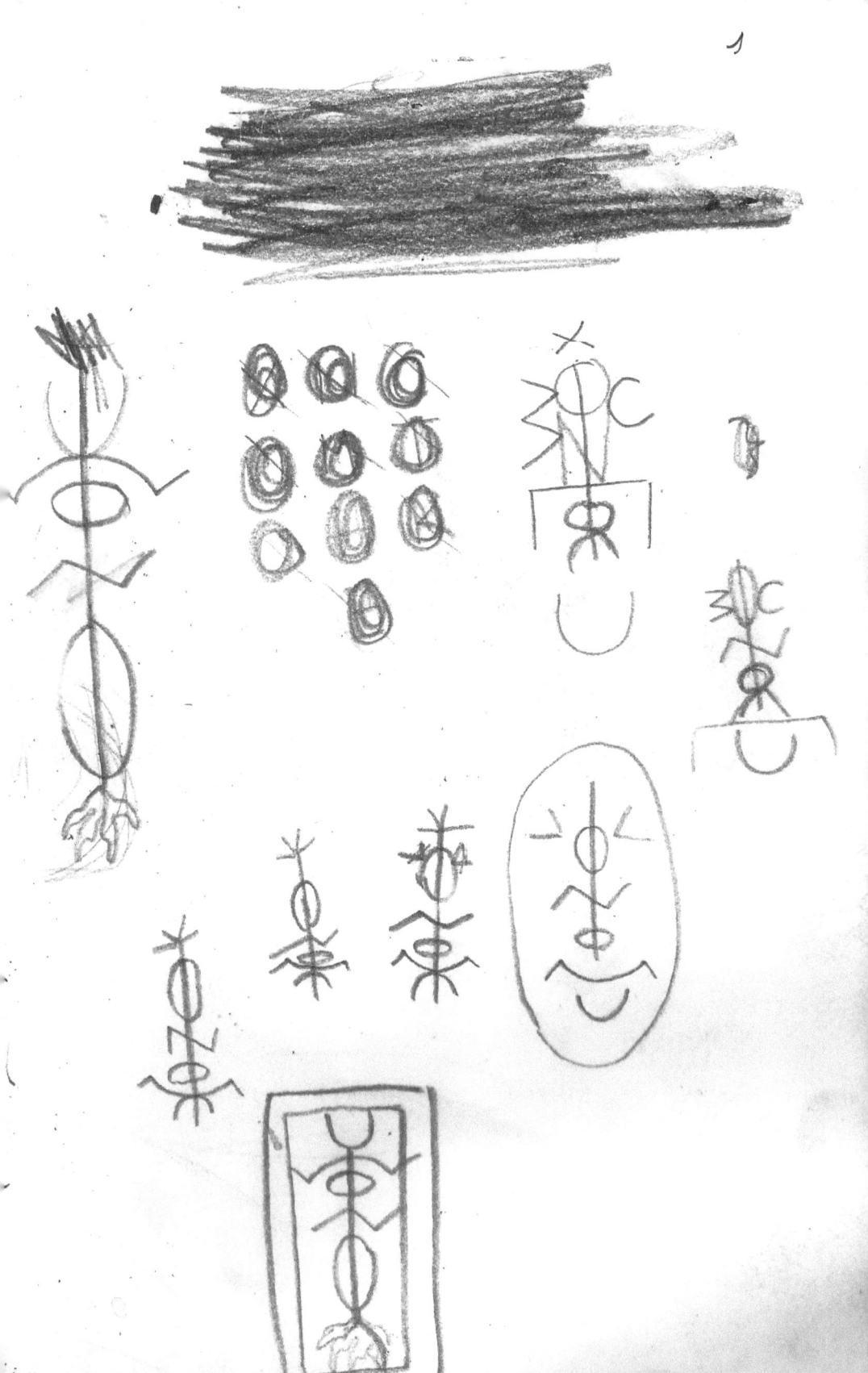

THE DEPLORABLE WORD
SINISTER

The first book to inform my paintings in a sinister direction was Richard Cavendish's The Black Arts. I ran across it quite by accident in the very back, hidden area of my college's library next to dusty outdated volumes of social statistics. It caught my eye simply because it was in terrible shape, barely held together by clear tape and some pages already making their way out of the binding. I distinctly remember holding the modestly sized book in my hand and seeing the already dim library lights flicker and shut off. I checked the book out and returned to my studio where I read the entire volume backwards, a strange habit I have. This was in 2008 when my paintings were developing into an oddly psychedelic and blasphemous direction. I was forced to return the book to the library after three weeks, and continued to look for anything that could guide me closer to essence of the occult that was now interesting me more and more. A close friend (whom I am now married to) found a 1967 copy of the book at a record store and gave it to me as a gift. I took this gesture seriously and began to use symbols more readily in my paintings. The next series of paintings I made were bizarre; women in pornographic poses with predatory animal heads, pentagrams hidden behind melting colors, eyes and teeth and horns everywhere. One of my paintings, which had the words *spread your legs for Satan* scrawled under a woman with two snakes curling inside her was hung in a school curated show. It was hung in a prominent place and I watched from across the room as people looked and then tried to get away from the painting as if it were a plague. People who pointed towards it were hushed and pushed aside. This was the first indication that I was making work that elicited a strong reaction, a reaction not of my own making. After reluctantly donning the title of Satanist, I was free to explore all matter of sinister aesthetics. I began to see myself and my work as a conduit for the essence of Satan. I set up an appropriate atmosphere in my small corner studio; I had a large tv brought in so that I could watch pornography and foreign horror films as I painted, listened to deafening heavy metal and practiced painting with both hands and my eyes closed while chanting. All of this inevitably lead to stranger and more intense paintings of melted orgies and symbols of ancient magick painted in the background.

Over the next few years I focused more on meditation and the actual development of magickal skills. After some consideration I became fully nocturnal and felt that true reality lay not in the living, waking world but in the strange states of trance like meditation I achieved in front of my large altar. I spent all my energy on this endeavor and refused to work a job or be distracted by anything which obviously had its price. I could no longer reap the benefits of money, society or the daylight. I found that living in squats and empty warehouses helped my craft. Even if it was not fit for human habitation, it was fit for habitation of another kind. I tattooed sigils and strange words on anyone who had the balls to get a tattoo in an abandoned building. I spent nights with my large Rottweiler in the overgrown graveyards of the various cities in which I lived. Magick began to work and I stopped reading the expensive books I had

THE DEPLORABLE WORD

bought myself. I had visions of symbols and painted them on all the walls and work surfaces I could find. I made as many altars as I could, leaving out raw red meat and cups full of graveyard dirt mixed with buried bones and salt as offerings. The flies that followed were welcomed guests of decay and I learned to sleep with their constant buzzing and the emerging white of their maggot offspring.

During this time, despite my efforts to find another who worked like me, I could find only people who lived relatively normal lives. Other Satanists shared my affinity for graveyards but recoiled at my suggestion of blood sacrifice. Some others wanted pictures of vaguely satanic rites and were confused by my aggression at the idea of photographing such a sacred rite. I could find no others who shared my vision of Satan as the great evil darkness that binds all things, more ancient than creation. I was invited to coven meetings that were nothing more than friends drinking wine on a full moon while on their phones. These experiences lead me to question the very word Satanism and its context in the spiritual realm. I began a lengthy research into ancient cults in search for some parallel. I found it in the forbidden rites of the Aztecs, a most feared people. I found it in the Mesopotamian primordial myth and in the Egyptian hatred of Set. I came to understand that the word Satan is simply a contemporary stand-in for something much darker that remains hidden to those whose ego shields their vision. This path that is opened by Satan is winding and treacherous and eventually leads into something that even Satan cannot completely engulf. Through research and intense ritual experimentation I found that there was another, greater something. This was spoken about only in the context of a warning: Do Not Enter. All cultures have forbidden rites and rituals. They are forbidden for a reason – it opens a gateway for the enemy of all creation. Not even the cruelest and most bloodthirsty of ancient priests would utter its name in the night. The risk is clear – insanity, violence and disease are its harbingers.

All of this culminated during the Blood Moon eclipse which happened to be the night of my 30th birthday. I do not celebrate my birth, but the timing seemed auspicious. I watched the full red moon slide into darkness while seated on a rusting piece of metal next to the barbed wire fences that lined the property in which I lived and worked. A heavy feeling came over me as I watched my husband start to slip into sleep on my lap. We slept hard that night. After awakening the next morning something was different. Without even thinking, I rearranged my entire altar, discarding many of my most prized objects. All that was left was a small cauldron, some black candles and many mirrors. One month later, during all hallows eve, I fasted for three days while working on a large magick circle and four collages. At the time, I actually disliked the idea of collage, I felt it was an inferior medium. I reluctantly obeyed this change of direction and worked on somehow combining cut images with hand-drawn sigils for LEVIATHAN, LUCIFER, BEAL and BELIAL for the series. I had never used a permanent circle but now I found myself painting a thick black ring on a filthy beige rug in my studio. Around the ring I wrote in my personal font of ghostlike squirming

THE DEPLORABLE WORD

letters ZAZAS ZAZAS NASATANADA ZAZAS on one side of the circle and the same words backwards on the other side. I placed the four collages at the four corners of the rug and sat in the middle. After using this circle consistently, others who came into my studio would step around it. I used it for meditation and as a seat of power in which to receive visions. Eventually, I slid the carpet under my workspace so that I was always seated in the middle. The art that I was making didn't look like my previous work at all. It was a completely new way of working, an amalgamation of learned technical art skills and the blackest magick I could channel. I realized the knife I was using for the bloodletting portions of my rituals was quickly being replaced with my Xacto blade which I was using to cut collage pieces causing every piece to contain my blood. Because of this exchange of fluids my hands became useful extensions of some unknown force. This did not feel the same as my satanic rituals, all of which essentially ended in a fulfillment of some material ends, Satan being lord of this world. An almost alien comprehension of images and symbols began to grow inside my creative instincts. I worked only at night on the heart of the pieces and left the menial sketching and manual labor aspect of art making for the daylight. I started referring to this as the day shift and the night shift. Late at night I could see shadows changing the configuration of the work and faces appeared which I traced over in order to preserve them. Even the way in which my hands moved over the paper was different. I didn't leave the studio for months and stopped communicating to the outside world about anything except the work. The habit of awaking in the night to sketch or write down messages developed. My sketchbook contents began to make me seem more like a serial killer than an artist. I found that I was writing backwards and mirrored text. A new system of magick was dissolving the divide between art and ritual.

States of possession became more pronounced after the eclipse. While I would try to fight it before, using breathing techniques to slow my heart-rate, now I don't bother. This state is usually provoked by feelings of anxiety, aggression, depression or conflict. It slips in sideways while I am distracted by my human emotions and takes over my muscles first. My entire body tightens, twisting my small figure into odd shapes. I can feel my hands becoming rigid and tight claws, my spine rejecting the lower half of my body leaving my legs to kick violently away. My husband, who has been present through many of these escalating states tells me later that my eyes become wild and extremely dilated, my movements like an animal on full alert. My voice changes to a raspy growl and I snap and bite at any flesh within my reach. Even with considerable weight on me I can still thrash free of him. These states last anywhere from thirty minutes to an entire night. I do not remember all of the states, I am somewhere else and have only a vague dreamlike understanding of what is occurring. Although my eyes are usually shut tight, if I get a glimpse of the world it looks as though I am underwater and everything is murky. I can tell it is over when my breathing changes back and I again feel the flood of human emotions again. The possessions aren't joyous or blissful experiences, they are exhausting and take a huge toll on me. However, I see now that these states are a necessary contact with the

THE DEPLORABLE WORD

THE DEPLORABLE WORD

Abyss. It allows me to be used in its name which is all an evil artist could ask for. The black magick worked with the energies of the Abyss is extremely potent and does not have any semblance of compassion, even for its most dedicated and talented agents. Unlike the magick worked in the name of Satan, it does not have a component of indulgence or hedonism. It does not revel in blasphemous acts like Satan, instead it is beyond all duality and human understanding. To dream even a sliver of the truth outside this cosmos is to be changed into something else entirely. Describing it as evil does not do it justice, it simply appears evil to those on the other side, those who value only the repetitive cycle of creation. I have come to see that Satan is the one who opens the path towards the Void. I remain in, as I have been chanting and hissing for a decade, *YID CHES MUN NAG LAM SET AN* – supreme dedication to the pitch black path of Satan. This path is made pitch black only by the overwhelming existence of the first and most ancient of all forces, that which shall not be named. The path ends in total dissolving of the spirit into the realms just beyond the edge of the cosmos, where the universe has yet to expand and the infinite terror waits. Escaping the cycle of life is not enough, one who worships the Abyss must see that all life is an error. To truly accept the will of the Abyss is to accept that the entirety of creation – anything outside the pure truth of the dark beyond the veil – is false.

THE DEPLORABLE WORD
COBALT AND COLLYRIUM

SATURDAY 9 JANUARY 2016.

Today Sarah and I met up for coffee at the Ash Street Café. Work had been busy for what seemed like months, and so I hadn't seen her for a while. It was great to sit together, even briefly, and to hear about her recent artistic projects. I could tell she'd been working that very day: she had taken time to put on her make-up and do her hair, but there were still flecks of teal and mauve paint on her fingers from some recent painting, which indicated that she'd washed in a hurry to meet me. Sarah was so happy and excited that one of the upscale galleries in town had just exhibited one of her installations, and there had been some very positive reactions to several of her more avant-garde pieces. In fact, as I ordered some coffee and chocolate cake for us both, she proudly stated that coffee was her treat since she was "flush" with cash. I was so happy to see her finally getting some recognition from the artistic community. Sarah had always been so talented, but the art scene was hard to break into, especially in the faltering economic times which the state was suffering. But somehow, she'd gotten the contact info from a friend of a friend of a gallery owner, and after a series of what seemed to be positive coincidences, she finally had her first big exhibit. I cursed myself inwardly for not having been able to attend, but she didn't seem to mind.

Most importantly, she said that one of the gallery patrons had been really impressed with her work, and had commissioned her to do a series of paintings for him. She described him as a man in his mid-fifties, dressed formally in a grey suit and a lean, pale face that was almost blue from the razor. Sarah had gotten the impression that he was some kind of religious figure – not because he was wearing the white collar, but rather that he had a slightly distant yet kindly look, which one tends to see in the clerical vocation. She found him staring at one of the smaller pieces in the gallery, a painting she had done for a friend based on an astral reading. The painting showed a normal face surrounded by a writhing mass of shadows. The man in grey had stared intently at it for nearly half an hour, while the exhibit bustled around him.

Finally, wondering if he wanted to acquire the piece, Sarah had approached him and asked if she could help him. She'd shaken hands with him, which was awkward for a moment as he had been holding some papers rolled up, much like a newspaper. He introduced himself, and of course she'd forgotten his name immediately – it was maybe something Italian or French. The gentleman smiled warmly and expressed great interest in her work. He praised the exhibit, citing several examples of her work around the room that had really impressed him the most. He told Sarah that he certainly wanted to support her work, and so he wondered if she might accept a commission to do several paintings for his study. He could pay well for her time, he hastened to add, and if she accepted, he insisted on giving her two (or three) grand up front to cover immediate costs. Sarah couldn't believe her good fortunate – she'd sold works before, but usually for

THE DEPLORABLE WORD

several hundred at most.

"The only stipulation," he had said, "Is that I'd really like you to do the paintings as a reaction to some esoteric papers that I've been translating from a medieval text known as *The Deplorable Word*. I'd give you a few pages to read each week, and you'd paint whatever you *feel* from reading them."

Sarah's work was esoteric art, and so she'd readily agreed. He'd given her the roll of papers in his hand, which was comprised of only a few pages. Then he removed a slim black wallet from his coat, and counted out thirty crisp hundred-dollar bills. He gave them to her with all the ease of someone sharing a cup of coffee. Sarah tried to accept the money with candor, but was worried that she had looked nervous. He then took one last look around the gallery, shook hands with her again gravely (but not unkindly), and said he'd check a week later to see how the first of the series was progressing.

Sarah told me that she'd already spent a third of the cash on supplies for the project — canvases, brushes, new paints, and a fresh smock. She'd spent the morning getting the studio ready, and now after having coffee with me, she planned to return home and start by reading the first batch of translated pages. It was so nice to see her so excited, and I was secretly relieved that she wouldn't be a "starving" artist, at least not as long as she had this particular project to work on. She was still in her early twenties, and I expected that if a career as an artist didn't work out, she had plenty of time to try other projects before the financial pressures of a house or mortgage began to close in.

We finished the chocolate cake in silence, and then made some small talk about our shared lack of social lives. She muttered something about a date with some musician named Trent, from a death-metal band she'd been following, but it hadn't gone anywhere. Sarah had always been quite attractive when she'd let herself been seen, but she has a habit of remaining unseen, as if light bent away from her by design. Her biggest obstacle to relationships of any kind was that her only true love was her art — she'd often stay in on the weekends and work obsessively on her music or painting. I'd call three or four times a day for an entire week without her picking up the phone, so sometimes I'd just drop by to make sure that she was ok. Invariably she would be fine, but she'd be so absorbed in her work that she had just lost track of time. So I hoped that this particular project would be a good one, because most of her art was only appreciated by a few old friends like myself. If this patron liked her work, maybe it would mean other (paying) contracts. I really hoped so, because it would mean that her art could remain her livelihood, and no one wanted that more than her.

True to her word, Sarah insisted on getting the check. She gave me a hug, and then we both departed the café. It was good to see her feeling so positive.

SATURDAY 16 JANUARY 2016.

Today I waited nearly 20 minutes for Sarah at the Ash Street Café, but she finally arrived with a breathless apology. She was smiling, but she had heavy, dark circles under her eyes, and she'd clearly not

mindful + conscious
breathing

I LOVE YOU

CANCER

SEAMLESS
INTEGRATION
WITH
ALL
FEAR
AND
EMPTY
SPACE

fear not, for I am not forgetting
you, I ask only to obliterate
the cells of humanity since
you and cleanse you of this
infected nomor.
do not allow life to fester.
watch it clear and flow
within the fluids

THE DEPLORABLE WORD

had time to put on any make-up to hide them. Sarah told me that she'd worked all the way through the night, in fact for several nights, and she'd finally fallen asleep in a chair in the studio. She would have slept right through our coffee date, except that the phone had rang (a wrong number, it turned out), and she'd only had moments to change her clothes, splash some water on her face, and run to catch the bus. I had brought my laptop to work while I was waiting, so I didn't tease her too badly for almost standing me up. I had planned to order the usual coffee and chocolate cake for us both, but she uncharacteristically said she was hungry and ordered coffee and a sandwich instead.

Sarah exhibited that nervous, jittery energy that I'd seen in her when she was disturbed from working. She didn't even ask how I was, she just started into a rushed monologue about how good it felt to be working on this project. The pages she'd gotten from the gentleman in grey were some kind of origin myth, describing the world in ages past, when it had all been an "Abyss" of black mists, chaos, and grinding ice. There had been shapeless things that moved through that murk, and it sounded like a fairly awful kind of place to me. Sarah, however, seemed to relish the story, and she described it so vividly that I got chills as if the dark fog of the place were momentarily around me.

"You should see what I've painted so far," she exclaimed, "It's like a mix of hues I'd never thought to put together. It just seemed like it would be, well, fucking *wrong* to just splash black all over the canvas. I mean, the image calls for some sophistication, something deeper. So, I've been experimenting with different hues and media to see how best to make it come alive, you know?"

I did not quite understand, and it must have shown on my face.

"Well..." Sarah paused, "the Abyss isn't just black, it's the end of color and light and sound, or maybe it's the source. I mean, how do you depict something that is prior to existence itself? It's not *real* or *unreal*, it's something (or somewhere) that doesn't distinguish between those states. So I can't just use black by itself. I'm mixing several shades of grey, black, teal, greens, reds. It needs to look fluid, like it's in perpetual motion."

"So you're saying that you're trying to draw supernatural darkness?" I asked.

"No," she corrected, "it's *preternatural* darkness, and I'm painting it, not drawing it."

"Supernatural, preternatural, what's the difference?" I asked.

She waved a hand distractedly as if it was obvious.

"Well, 'supernatural' means 'above nature', or 'superior to nature.' So a ghost, a zombie, an angel, they're all supernatural. Magick is supernatural, because it bends the natural order. But 'preternatural' means 'prior to nature', or 'it was fucking here before the cosmos.'"

"Doesn't Ann Rice use the term 'preternatural' sometimes for her vampires?" I suddenly remembered seeing the word when I'd borrowing *Interview with a Vampire* from her a couple summers ago.

THE DEPLORABLE WORD

"Yeah, true" she nodded, "But she uses the term wrongly. If it's born, lives, or dies, or won't stay dead, it's supernatural. But if it pre-dates the universe, then you call it preternatural."

"Occult nerd," I teased her, and she playfully punched me in the arm.

Sarah ran her hands through her long hair several times, brushing it back away from her face. I knew her well enough to know that the gesture meant she was thinking about her work.

"So are you enjoying the work?" I asked.

"Hell yeah," she nodded, "This is the best project I've ever worked on. The client is dropping off the next set of pages tomorrow, so I'm kinda looking forward to seeing those. It's like illustrating a story, one chapter at a time. I just can't stop painting, not even for breaks. It's like the painting is already done and I'm just recreating it."

"That's fantastic!" I said, "Sounds like you're really hitting your stride. But what do you say to taking a break, maybe seeing a movie with me tonight? There's a midnight showing of that new indy horror film 'Nine Angles', you said you wanted to see it, remember? If you've been working nonstop, maybe a night off will help recharge your creative batteries. Heck, do it for me, I've been killing myself at work and I really could us the break. Just a few more hours – you can do it!" I smiled my most winning smile.

I thought she'd say "no", because she started to frown. But then, maybe seeing me looking slightly worried, she surprised me by brightening up and agreeing to come. We finished our snack and then I hailed us a cab. The movie wasn't bad, and it was nice to have the company. I hated weekends with nothing to do, and I secretly hoped that the fresh air and society would help Sarah from becoming a total shut in. It was a good night, and it felt good even for me to have something fun to do on an otherwise lonely Saturday night.

FRIDAY 22 JANUARY 2016.

After not answering her phone for five days, Sarah actually called me for a change! She said that she hadn't had time to get groceries for a few days, and asked if I could pick up a few simple things and bring them by the apartment. I was happy to do it, and it would give me a chance to see whatever she'd been working on. I'd spoken to her last on Sunday, the day right after the movie, and she'd been excited about the new pages she'd gotten. The client had them delivered by a courier, and she'd devoured them and thrown herself right back into the work. I did want to see her, I was already dog-tired from work this week; a tight-deadline had cost me a few night's sleep, so part of me just wanted to go home and sleep – but instead I took a cab to the nearest grocery store to get her some supplies.

Sarah lived in a low-income part of town, where one found squat condominiums with cheap rent, bad landlords, and a very mixed quality of neighbors. Sarah lived on the fourth floor of one such colorful building, and whenever I stepped inside, it seemed like the air smelled of old cigarettes and urine. I climbed the stairs and made my way down the dimly-

THE DEPLORABLE WORD

lit hallway that lead to Sarah's flat. I rang the doorbell and waited. I could hear the low drone of industrial music from inside, and so I had to ring the doorbell a few more times before she heard me. When she opened the door, she was dressed in a white t-shirt and jeans, both of which were liberally smeared with various colors of paint, despite the use of a smock. The hallway of the apartment building had poor lighting, but it seemed as if a thick sheen of sweat was over her face, as though she'd been exerting herself. As the door opened she appeared momentarily confused, as if she'd forgotten that I was coming. But when she saw it was me, she smiled warmly, and reached up to hug me. She kissed my cheek briefly, and I was a little alarmed at how warm she felt.

She took me by the arm and pulled me into her small apartment. Sarah lived in a claustrophobic bachelor flat which had only a bathroom, a kitchenette, and small living room which doubled as her studio. The entryway was dimly lit, so I had to be careful not to trip as we entered into the studio itself. Sarah usually slept on a futon in the studio, and it was the only room of the house with decent lighting. When we entered, I saw that there were a number of covered paintings that were strewn about the room.

"Are you running a fever?" I asked with some concern. Normally she was always very clean (if disheveled), but now her hair looked almost greasy, as if she hadn't showered in several days.

"What? No! Well, maybe? Am I? Umm, I can't tell, but I think I feel fine. Don't I look fine?" she asked with some confusion. She turn towards me then, brushing the hair away from her face, and the light of the studio caught in her eyes. I was struck by two thoughts: one, that in the moment, she looked stunning – there was a wild glittering in her eyes that made her light up the room for an instant. Her art truly did transform her into a different person. But my other thought was that something was really wrong with her. She really did have a sheen on her skin, and the scent of the room was somehow sour. Sarah didn't seem to understand why I was there, and she'd called me only an hour earlier. And she'd managed, somehow, to smear some faint traces of black paint on part of her hair and scalp. I moved the one small window in the apartment and opened it a crack to let some fresh air in. The January air was chilly, and she shivered.

"*Seo ǽgrynde is swiðe fǽrlíce*" she muttered distractedly, and then she started to cough.

"What's that?" I asked.

"What's what?" she said, looking quizzically at me.

"You just said something in German, I think" I said.

She scoffed. "You're hearing things, I was just clearing my throat."

Frowning, I carried the groceries to the little kitchenette, and started to put them in the fridge. "I think you have a fever," I began, "do you have any Tylenol or Aspirin I can get for you?"

"No, no, I'm fine, just need to sleep," she said. And she looked it, she really looked physically exhausted. Her

THE DEPLORABLE WORD

eyes, however, kept darting around between the various covered canvases in the room.

"Can I, uh, see what you've been working on?" I asked hesitantly.

"Oh! Oh yes! Sorry, of course!" She beamed at me, and moved to remove the cover from the first painting.

The cover came off, and it took a moment to understand what the image was. At first, I thought it was the image of an oily black lake, but on inspection the color was actually closer to cobalt, that shade of blue that is so dark that it almost hurts the eyes to stare at for so long. The surface seemed almost to ripple like water, and as the light and shadows of the room moved across it, it almost seemed alive. Somehow, Sarah had managed to cast it in such a way that it drank in the light from the room – I would have sworn that when she pulled the cover off the thing, the room darkened slightly as if the room's luminescence were swallowed by the painting. In fact, the longer I stared at it, the more it seemed that the light did not dance across it – it was as if the light that shone on the image did not so much reflect on the oily surface, but rather struggled weakly on the surface before being pulled into the painting itself. She'd managed, somehow, to really make the painting seem alive. It suggested a certain sluggish malevolence, but there was nothing (absolutely nothing) static about that image.

"Gods, Sarah," I breathed. I genuinely had no idea she had possessed such talent.

"Do you like it?" she asked, standing beside me. I could feel the heat radiating from her, its intensity reminding me that I needed to get her to take the Tylenol before I left.

"I don't know if I *like* it, but – Jesus wept – it's fucking *brilliant*. How did you do it?"

She shrugged. "It took time. I made three more before it, but they didn't have the right, the right... fuck, the right resonance, you know? The early drafts were technically good, but not at all on the right frequency. I finally had to read the story again and again to get it so I could really see it. I mixed some different hues, new combinations I hadn't considered. I added things to the paint, different ingredients. I actually needed to order collyrium from the pharmacy. Hey, did you know that a gloss of human blood and machine oil produces the most incredible sheen?"

I was a bit startled – human blood? And what the hell was collyrium?

She kept talking, faster now. "I finally got the first one done, and then I started to work on the second painting. Gods, the dreams!" She barked, a sharp hard laughter I'd never heard from her before. "You can't do this stuff without dreams, you know? Crazy stuff, weird colors and shapes, I can't describe it very well." She straightened a little. "But I don't need to describe it, I just need to paint it."

Suddenly, she slumped, as if whatever force had gone out of her. She literally sagged against me, and I caught her.

"Sarah, you're not well, you need to rest. Here, come lie down." I half carried

THE DEPLORABLE WORD

her to the mattress on the ground. I kicked the covers off and got her to lie down. She seemed already half asleep, and her eyes closed immediately. I pulled the smock off her, and covered her with the sheets and blanket. She shivered, despite the relative warmth of the room. So I went and searched the bathroom cabinet for the Tylenol, and poured her a glass of water. With some difficulty, I got her awake enough to take the medicine and most of the water too. Next, I went to the kitchen and made her a sandwich, which I wrapped it in plastic and put on a plate. I peeled an orange too. Somewhere in the studio I managed to find a pen and some paper. I wrote, *Please eat something. Drink water. Call me in the morning.* I put the note, the sandwich plate, and the orange next to her mattress. Something was very wrong here, but I couldn't explain it, and God knows I was already tired from my own work week. Should I have stayed? Maybe, but there was nowhere to lie down, the place was so tiny, I would have had to sleep on the floor. I didn't know what else to do, so I checked her one last time; she seemed to be deep asleep, so I quietly left the apartment and headed home.

FRIDAY 5 FEBRUARY 2016, 6:30 PM.

When I'd seen Sarah two weeks prior, she'd been a bit manic, unwashed, and feverish. But she didn't seem seriously ill, I mean, she just seemed to be experiencing the side-effects of someone who's been working obsessively indoors without enough sunlight and nutrition. I'd seen her like this before, some years ago when she'd been depressed, but back then she'd just become catatonic for days on end. Now, catatonic was the last thing she could be accused of – she was more like a force a nature that didn't know when to stop. On the bright side, surely the client only wanted a limited number of paintings, and so (I hoped) that when the job finished, she'd go back to a more normal pace of work. Maybe, I mused, she needed to be a little crazy to actually finish the job. Hadn't some famous painter like Van Gough cut off an ear? Artists were already unstable, it was practically part of the basic criteria in order to actually make art.

But two weeks had rolled by, and she'd missed or ignored almost all of my calls. When she did answer, it was usually to rant about her commission and the latest batch of papers she'd gotten, and the impact they were having on her work. "The dreams," she said, "they're so vivid, I can literally see what the texts call 'the Shapeless Ones' in the black mists. God, you should see them," and she'd shudder and start coughing for a moment on the other end of the phone.

Today she had let me get her out of the apartment once, and it was just to get supplies. There was an art shop up on the fifth that she liked, and so I hailed a cab to take us there. She'd dressed warmly, since it was February, but she shivered despite the coat, hat, and scarf. She'd seemed skittish and avoided looking at me – I could hardly get her to speak. But at least she was outside of the apartment, and it meant that she was getting some sun. After I pleaded with her, she agreed to stop for a proper meal before heading home. We went to the usual Ash Street Café, and I ordered a soup and sandwich for us both. She didn't

THE DEPLORABLE WORD

even seem to notice when the waiter came to ask what we wanted. She sat there and stared out the window, without giving any sign that she'd contracted the manic fever that had possessed her that last several weeks.

But after she'd eaten, she seemed to loosen up a little. The waiter brought us two steaming mugs of hot chocolate after the meal, and Sarah seemed to relish the hot drink. Maybe it was the warmth, but after she'd drained half the mug, she looked at me and smiled. A real smile, the *real* her, not the weird ecstatic thing that had taken her place these past few weeks. She shyly told me that the client had dropped by to inspect the work, and he'd given her another five thousand dollars as an advance. Five thousand! My jaw must have dropped, because she started to laugh, and then I started to laugh too. I knew her work was good, but that was serious money! I called for a second round of hot chocolate so we could drink to her professional success.

At this point, between the food and the warmth of the drink, she had some color back in her cheeks. We got the cab back to her building. I offered to carry the art supplies upstairs, but she insisted she could do it herself. She'd smiled like her old self, and told me that it felt nice to be out of her studio, and that I needed to make sure to come over more often and drag her out, if she didn't answer the phone. I told her I was sorry I couldn't do so more often, it was just my own job that had kept me so busy. We both agreed to be better. I left feeling happy to have seen her actually doing better.

WEDNESDAY 10 FEBRUARY 2016.

Oh hell. Fucking hell. I'm not writing any more after this.

I got home from work tonight, and found that I had several missed calls on my phone. They were all from Sarah, and so I called her back right away. It rang once, twice, and then she picked up. At least, I think she answered, but she didn't speak. There was only a strange noise in the background, I couldn't quite hear it, but it sounded like several animals (bulls? whales?) voices lowing or groaning at odd intervals. It had a certain rhythmic quality to it. I started shouting, but she didn't answer. So I hung up, and got my coat. I ran downstairs to the street and waved frantically for a cab.

It took several minutes to find a taxi, but eventually I did get one, and then it was just another twenty minutes to her building. There was an ambulance outside taking away some rangy youth dressed in ragged blacks and greys; his swollen face was terribly blue and purple as though he'd suffered some kind of blunt force trauma. Strange – normally people got shot or knifed, but this had always been a rough neighborhood. I pushed past the small crowd of people crowding around the ambulance and began to make my way upstairs. As I neared Sarah's floor, I could faintly hear that strange droning noise which I'd heard over the phone. There was something about hearing it again that made my stomach feel slightly queasy. It wasn't the loudness of the sound – I could only barely hear it – it was the weirdness of it that made my insides hurt. I ignored the nausea and walked quickly to her door.

possession is nine tenths of
LIFE IS
THE HOAX

civilization is a hoax
sell us ...
solar ...
assisting gerald ford

red and teal

phemail

CIELO
paradise
heaven sky

PW peter weibel
Observation of the observation
1973

WAR VIBES
abeausoleil
hy...

WITCH PRGA

Hee
SUGAR
colonialism → VOODOO

CM
JFK
MLL
ONLY
Sirhon Sirhan
anti israel

THE DEPLORABLE WORD

The weird noise was louder here, it sounded like she was playing some new form of experimental grey noise I hadn't heard before.

I realized, when I got to her door, that it was actually slightly ajar. There wasn't much light coming from inside. I knocked on the door. "Sarah? Sarah?" I called, but my voice seemed muted by the weird noise that droned inside. I tried to knock on the door, but the force of my hand just pushed the door open further. So I entered Sarah's room, and the droning noise stopped. No, I realized, it had not stopped – it had muted somewhat, its volume reduced, but the sound was still there. The other thing I noticed is that it was surprisingly cold and damp in her apartment. I couldn't find the light switch, and the dim glare from the hallway didn't seem to really reach into the apartment itself. I called her again. "Sarah?" This time I heard her, faintly, murmuring in reply. I stepped forward into the murk, the only light in the studio coming from bright street lights that shone dully through the one lone window. I could hear Sarah murmuring in the darkness of the room, but it was so oppressively dark that I could hardly see.

I knew where the lights where in the studio, and so I slowly felt my way across the room to where the switch would be on the wall. I nearly tripped over something in the dark and stumbled, but I kept my balance. It was fucking *cold*. The odd droning noise seemed to be all around me, and it was beginning to give me a headache. I found the switch and turned on the lights.

It would be wrong to say that the room actually brightened, but the oppressiveness of the darkness certainly seemed to recede. The bulb in the middle of the ceiling began to flicker sullenly, and at first I still couldn't see anything. It was like the darkness had swallowed the room itself, and I had the sudden sensation that I was standing in the midst of a misty, tenebrous tunnel. Swathes of shadow seemed to swim at the edges of my field of vision, and I could see and feel the black mists of the place swirling around me. Any sense of the studio was entirely gone, and the one lone light in the ceiling did not so much give me light, as it allowed me to see how the studio was no longer properly a studio.

Then the bulb brightened, just a little, but it was enough to see that it was still the studio. The paintings had been removed, piled likely in a closet, and the room stood empty. But the entire room – the walls, the ceiling, the floor – had all been painted with that cobalt slime that I'd first seen on the first painting. It fucking glistened, and it seemed to swallow whatever light shone from the flickering bulb.

It took a moment, but I found Sarah. Despite the cold, she was only half-dressed, wearing only a pair of drab boxer shorts and a white t-shirt. She was standing pressed up against the wall, her face and body literally pressing against the surface. She seemed to be covered in the paint – it covered her arms and legs, as if hundreds of blackish-blue hands had clutched at her. Even her hair seemed stained with the cobalt paints. From where I was standing, it looked oddly like the wall was bulging slightly around her, as if she was pressing into it instead of against it. "Sarah!" I cried, and

THE DEPLORABLE WORD

she stirred slightly, murmuring against the wall. Was she sleep walking? I cross the room and tried to grab her, but my hand slipped on the paint when I tried to pull her around. I grabbed her then, forcefully, and the droning noise in the room shot up. It sounded angrier, like a swarm of immense writhing things, spiraling around us in the murk. But I didn't care about the noise, I was terrified for her.

Sarah shuddered in my grasp, but allowed herself to be turned around. Her entire front had been smeared with the paint, all but her face, which was merely smudged. Her eyes were unfocused at first, like someone who is drugged, but then they found my face and she smiled. It was a wide, delirious smile. "You came," she breathed, "Can you hear them?"

"Sarah, I'm getting you out of here," I said in a harsher voice than I intended. She flinched back away from me.

"No," she said, "this is my... I'm home, this is where... it feels *so good* to be here." She gestured around the room. "Do you like it? Can you see it? Can you see them?"

"This is, well, this isn't *right*, Sarah! What are you doing here?" I shook my head. "Get some clothes, you're staying at my place, or I can take you to your mom's if you prefer. I am not leaving you here alone again!"

She stepped back from me. "I'm not alone. Can't you hear them singing? I'll never be alone again."

Then I saw the blood stain on her t-shirt, red against the white cloth and blackish paint. She saw me staring at it, and she smiled.

"My musician friend, Trent, he dropped by earlier. He didn't like the work and he tried to take me away."

"What happened to him? What did you do?" I asked with a growing sense of dread now replacing the nausea.

"Me? Nothing! But the shadows in the walls, they didn't like him at all. I – I don't remember. Did you see him?" She shook her head. "I think maybe they made him go away."

That lanky fellow in black being loaded into the ambulance. His face had been completely unrecognizable. Had she done that? If not, who else – what else could have done it?

I couldn't bring myself to believe it. Despite the weirdness of the sounds that emanated from the walls (*grey noise*, my subconscious insisted shrilly, *it's just music, has to be music*) and the odd way that the shadowy streams of the painting seemed to writhe of their own accord, I just could not accept that there was anything supernatural happening.

"Sarah, you've just been reading too much into those pages – it's just a myth, it's not real."

She looked disappointed in me, then she grinned suddenly at me, as if I was playing some joke.

"You can hear them, can't you?" she asked. "You can hear them singing in the mists. They're so cold, their touch burns." She glanced down at her hands, as if they too had been burned. I couldn't tell, because she was covered in cobalt paint to the forearms.

"Look," I said sternly, "You're leaving here. Pack a bag, I'm dragging you out of here by force if I have to. Maybe it's the fumes, but you're acting crazy."

She stood suddenly and put her arms around me, burying her face in my chest.

THE DEPLORABLE WORD

Her hair smelled of that odd, briny paint, but it felt good to hold her for a moment. But gods, she was cold. There was no fever this time, it was like holding a corpse. I didn't like the feeling;

"I know you mean well," she murmured against me, "You've always been so sweet. I wish I could bring you with me, but they won't hold the tunnel open long enough for two to make the journey. The client, it's all he wanted, he just wanted the passage. But I can't make this and let another go, I need to see, I need to know. I can't get their music out of my head. He'll have to find another artist."

"Sarah, we can discuss this at your mom's place. Or maybe the hospital."

I suddenly realized: *the ambulance*. If I hurried downstairs, I could catch the paramedics before they left with the wreckage of the musician.

I pulled away from her cold embrace, and gently brushed the hair away from her eyes. She looked oddly peaceful, and smiled at me in that weird, drugged way.

"Stay here, I'm just going to be downstairs for a moment. I'll be right back, don't go anywhere, ok?" I asked her, as gently as I could.

Sarah stood on her toes and pressed her cold lips briefly against my cheek. Then she gestured around herself almost helplessly and said, "Where would I go? I'm already almost home."

"Ok great – be right back," I muttered, and I headed for the door. It closed behind me when I stepped into the hallway. I headed down the stairs, praying the paramedics would still be there.

They had gone. *Fuck*. I could see the red lights of the ambulance receding in the distance. The crowd of onlookers was stating to disperse. "Never seen nothing like it, 'e was torn like a rag doll," I overheard one elderly lady remark to her neighbor. No way, absolutely no way Sarah had done that. I suddenly wondered why I thought it had been ok to leave her in the room.

Grudgingly, I turned and made my way back up the stairs. As I neared the top floor, that strange droning noise began to rise, reaching a vibrating crescendo that made my teeth hurt. Then before I could reach Sarah's door, the noise stopped entirely. As my hand reached out for the door knob, there was silence within.

I opened the door and stepped inside. The oppressive gloom had faded considerably, and now even the dim lights from the hallway had no trouble giving enough illumination for me to see into the apartment. The chill had also noticeably diminished, in fact the room was only slightly cooler than the hallway, and there was no trace at all of the misty dampness I had felt only minutes earlier. The studio light was still on, and I called out.

"Sarah? Sarah are you ready to go?"

Sarah didn't answer, and I couldn't hear her murmuring or moving around at all from the small entryway. I would have said that the apartment was almost too quiet, but in fact I could now hear the usual ambient noise from the tenants: television sets in the neighboring apartments, children crying upstairs, people arguing and shouting, and cars honking their horns on the street outside.

I stepped in the studio. The ceiling lightbulb no longer flicked: it shone dully

THE DEPLORABLE WORD

but brightly enough to give light to the entire room. The studio had shrank, somehow, back to its normal mundane dimensions. The walls, floor, and ceiling were still painted black, but there was nothing especially vibrant about the color. Only now could I see how she'd blended cobalt and collyrium in difference measures with teal, grey, and green. There were patches of blue and brown, ash, and redish smudges woven into the mix. In a sense, it was like she'd been weaving with color instead of painting. The work must have been painstaking, taking her days of labor to put it all together. There was still an oily sheen to the paint, but it seemed to be a basic gloss that one finds in fresh oil paintings. I could make out where she'd embedded bits of cloth and sand, maybe concrete power, into the mix, creating that odd rippling, three-dimension effect that had seemed to insinuate actual motion.

But there was something definitely different about the room. Before, it had really felt like more than just a painting. Steeping into that room had been like stepping into another place, not entirely in this world, and not fully in that Other Place that she had kept trying to tell me about.

The room was clean. There were no paintings there at all, maybe she'd burned them or else thrown them out. Maybe the client had taken them as collateral on his advances, I had no way to know. The only thing that had was left in the room was her mattress, stained with the smears and blemishes of the weeks' worth of paint. She'd clearly collapsed into bed countless times, too exhausted to wash off the paint and grime from her work.

The only thing out of place was her clothing. It was in a small pile against the place where she'd been pressed against the wall, the t-shirt collapsed messily atop her shorts. Even her underwear was there. What the hell? Where was she?

Frantic, I started shouting her name, but my voice now seemed deadened inside the room. I clutched my head, trying to think: where could she have gone? I would have seen her leave the building – there was only one set of stairs, and the window had no fire exit of any kind.

Then I heard the tiniest sound, a stirring, a scratching at the wall. I glanced sideways at the place where the sound had emanated from, and it seemed like for a moment, there was nothing new to see. Then I looked closer, I realized that the image had shifted. Now there was an impression in the paint. It was hard to describe. It looked like the like rough shape of a woman, almost invisible, swimming through the murk. She was surrounded by other shapes, which seemed to swim along side her, though it was hard to tell where she began and they ended. Or, maybe the woman was becoming one of the shadows. In either case, I'd have sworn that image was not there when I had spoken to Sarah just minutes earlier. Maybe I didn't look closely enough.

None of this made sense. I checked the bathroom (empty) and the kitchenette (also empty), and also the closet. It had her coat, boots, some empty canvases, but no sign of her old paintings. Even the pages that she'd gotten from the client seemed to have disappeared. The only evidence that she'd spent a month working on this insane project

THE DEPLORABLE WORD

was the fact that she'd completely plastered the studio walls and ceiling in thick coats of cobalt and collyrium, with rivulets of colors bleeding through the murk. Her clothes, her phone, even the money was still stuffed under her sleeping mattress. Where, hell, had she gone?

Or maybe: where? *Hell.* She had gone.

There was nothing to be done there, so I went home. I tried calling Sarah's mom, but she wasn't there. I tried the hospital, and when I didn't hear from her after a day, I contacted the police. They were entirely unsympathetic and even suggested I'd been somehow negligent in not having her committed to psychiatric care sooner. I even tried the gallery, to see if there was any record of the gentleman in grey, but the gallery director had no recollection of seeing Sarah with anyone of that description.

I don't know what to do. I checked with Sarah's landlord, and told him I'd cover the rent while Sarah is away traveling. Somehow, it didn't seem right to let anyone else in there. Maybe it would be dangerous to whatever new tenant. Worse, I was afraid that if they painted the walls back, I'd never see Sarah again.

I'm so afraid for her sake.

Sarah, *please* come back.

. – *FIN* –

THE DEPLORABLE WORD

THE DEPLORABLE WORD

THE DEPLORABLE WORD
THE ABYSS: A CONCISE HISTORY

The world of mythology is incredibly rich. In the ancient world, there was a very wide diversity in terms of how different cultures and religions conceived of the sacred and profane in all their manifestations, such as mortals, immortals, and the many realms of the cosmos. When one investigates ancient texts and traditions, the single most important feature one can hope to find is repetition. If a concept (i.e. a belief, a being, a myth) occurs in multiple cultures, then the scholar draws a large red circle around that concept, because its repeated occurrence is significant. Unless you can prove that some cultural contact occurred between the cultures in question, such shared traditions are usually based in a common experience. To give a simple example, most ancient cultures shared a belief that the sun was a benign deity, because they shared a common observation that the sun was a key part of agriculture. This being the case, most ancient cultures feature the sun as a being, a character that appears in the ancient stories. Contrariwise, most cultures do not share a myth about pink elephants, because they do not share a common observation of elephants, let alone pink elephants.

There are very few "shared observations" in ancient myth, and of course, almost all of them can be traced to direct experience of the natural world. Sickness, death, birth, gender – these are the sort of direct experience topics which find their way into common myths and legends. There is one exception to this rule, and it is quite disturbing. This exception is the common belief in the Abyss. By whatever name in the local language, the Abyss is a force of primordial darkness which defies almost all attempts to categorize it. It pre-dates the cosmos, which it appears to have vomited up or somehow borne. The Abyss is described by almost all cultures as a vast seething ocean of liquid darkness. It is chthonic, in that it lurks "beneath" the cosmos, which seems to have risen out of it. It is sentient, but its sentience is alien to the consciousness of gods and mortals. The Abyss is not alive or dead, but both of those concepts express aspects of it. It is described in almost every culture as being hostile to creation, and possessing a desire to maim and destroy entire universes, if roused to action.

THE ABYSS IN HINDU TRADITION

Take, for example, the ancient Rig Vedas of India, which date back to 2000 BCE. The 129th hymn of the Veda's 10th mandala reports:

नासदासीन्नो सदासीत्तदानीं नासीद्रजो नो व्योमा परो यत् ।
किमावरीवः कुह कस्य शर्मन्नम्भः किमासीद्गहनं गभीरम् ॥ १ ॥

Before time began, there was neither existence nor non-existence. There was no sky then, no the celestial realms beyond it. What covered it? Where was it? In whose keeping?
All was the Abyss, *in depths unfathomed.*

न मृत्युरासीदमृतं न तर्हि न रात्र्या अह्न आसीत्प्रकेतः ।
आनीदवातं स्वधया तदेकं तस्माद्धान्यन्न परः किञ्चनास ॥ २ ॥

THE DEPLORABLE WORD

Then there was neither death nor immortality, nor was there day or night. **The Abyss** *breathed without breathing – There was that One then, and there was no other.*

तम आसीत्तमसा गूह्ळमग्रे प्रकेतं सलिलं सर्वाऽइदम् ।
तुच्छ्येनाभ्वपिहितं यदासीत्तपसस्तन्महिनाजायतैकम् ॥३॥

At first there was only **Darkness** *wrapped in* **Darkness.**
All this was only **black water.** *That One which came to be, enclosed in nothing, arose at last, born of power.*

[...]

को अद्धा वेद क इह प्र वोचत्कुत आजाता कुत इयं विसृष्टिः ।
अर्वग्देवा अस्य विसर्जनेनाथा को वेद यत आबभूव ॥६॥

But, after all, who knows, and who can say Whence it all came, and how creation happened? The gods themselves are later than creation, so who knows truly whence it has arisen?

इयं विसृष्टिर्यत आबभूव यदि वा दधे यदि वा न ।
यो अस्याध्यक्षः परमे व्योमन्त्सो अङ्ग वेद यदि वा न वेद ॥७॥

The Abyss *is where the cosmos originated. Whether It fashioned it, or whether It did not, only* **the Abyss** *can tell – or perhaps even It cannot say.*

Thus, the most ancient sacred texts state clearly that the Abyss is darkness. Neither living nor dead, neither existing nor non-existing – neither a god, nor a place, nor an Entity, but something which is responsible for the origin of the entire cosmos. It was understood by the ancient Indians as a kind of black universe that generates gods and planets, and its sentience is so utterly alien to its creations that the Vedic sage wonders if it is even possible to communicate with such a force.

Sorcerers and demons are said to come from the Abyss, make use of its power, and return there at death. The Vedic scholar Norman Brown reports that:

> Those who reach this place are the actively anti-divine creatures. They are first of all Vṛtra, who as we have seen lies dead in that spot. All the asuras and dasyus are driven there (*adhamaṃ tamas*, AV. 9. 2. 18). Rakṣasas, if caught and attacked by the gods, perish and fall into that place, and those who employ rakṣasas; so, too, sorcerers.

It is worth adding that the Vedas state that the magick of sorcerers is derived from the power of the Abyss (here, Skt. *Asat*). Brown continues:

THE DEPLORABLE WORD

> These creatures go there because they operate with charms that are contrary to the ṛta (*ánṛtebhir vácobhiḥ*, stanza 8). They use charms that are *asat* "dealing with the non-existent" and conflict with charms that deal with the *sat* "the existent" (*sác cásac ca vácasī paspṛdhāte*, stanza 12).

So when magick is defined as the deliberate and willful *violation* of the cosmic order, it must be fueled by the Abyss, understood as the non-existent. To work magick is to draw the unreal into the real, and force a new existence by blending the two. The Abyss, then, is a mad realm of possibilities and clashing realities, and it is not a passive force. The Abyss can and does change reality when it is given the opportunity to do so. Thus speak the Vedas.

THE ABYSS IN CLASSICAL TRADITION

The ancient Hindu sages were not the only religious authorities to hold the belief that the Abyss was responsible for the cosmos. The Greeks and Romans likewise believed that this dreadful primordial Entity was at the heart of creation. The medieval author Boethius likewise records the existence of the classical Greco-Roman cult of the Abyss, under the composite name "Demogorgo", from Ancient Greek *daimon* "Entity" + *gorgo* "terrifying".[1] Boethius writes in the third preface of the *Geneneaology*:

> *Summa cum maiestate tenebrarum…veternosus ille deorum omnium gentilium proavus, undique stipatus nebulis et caligine, mediis in visceribus terre perambulanti michi comparuit Demogorgon, nomine ipso horribilis, pallore quodam muscoso et neglecta humiditate amictus, terrestrem tetrum fetidumque evaporans odorem, seque miseri principatus patrem potius alieno sermone quam suo confessus verbo.*

> That slumbering ancestor of all the pagan gods, surrounded everywhere by black mists and accompanied by the greatest majesty of darkness, appeared to me as I passed through the Abyss. **The Demogorgo** – that nameless horror! — shrouded in some kind of pale mucus and forgotten humidity, exhaling an earthy, monstrous, and bitter odor, stating with some kind of alien voice that it was the father of this miserable world. [translation mine]

It is clear from the Latin text that this Entity is not unknown to the ancient or medieval world, and that Christian mystics like Boethius had visions of it. It is described as being in a misty, murky darkness, and the notion of some black fluid is evident from the description. It speaks, but its voice is "alien", that is, not in any way

---

[1] See Jon Solomon, "Boccaccio and the Ineffable, Aniconic God Demogorgon". Cf. *The Devil's Quran*.

THE DEPLORABLE WORD

human. It is important to point out that Latin texts never descript angels or even the deity as "alien", because they are fundamentally cosmic entities.

The Boethian scholar Jon Solomon writes:

> Boccaccio actually quotes, namely, the invocation to an even more powerful supreme deity: [6.744-47]
>
>> Will you obey, or must he
>> Be summoned at the utterance of whose name the earth
>> Is always struck and trembles, who looks openly at the Gorgon,
>> And terrifies the Erinys when he whips her?[36]
>
> Although Boccaccio does not include them, the passage continues with several more relative clauses:
>
>> Who holds Tartarus unseen for you, whose
>> Upper gods you are, and who swears falsely by the Stygian waters?[37]
>
> This unnamed god of the netherworld does not have the characteristics of an Olympian god. Far from being anthropomorphic, the object of established cult, represented by a statue housed in a dedicated shrine or temple, associated with a specific ritual, or endowed with a function-specific power, this god is invisible, nameless, and endowed with ill-defined but extraordinary powers of evil. The mere utterance of his name can cause an earthquake, and he can look openly at the Gorgon and not turn to stone, whip the Erinyes who otherwise themselves lash their victims, and lie with impunity after swearing by Styx. And this nameless god dwells in a lower level of Tartarus in a sub-subterranean region. This part of the description is particularly important, for it marks a mid-first century *terminus post quem* for placing this nameless divinity with Demogorgonian features in the infernal regions.[38]

The Abyss and the Demogorgon are connected, as if the author has experinced the impersonal sentience of the Abyss and personified it as the Demogorgon. Bearing in mind that the human mind is not designed to apprehend or understand a force or Entity on such a scale, this is a reasonable reaction.

As Boethius describes, the Romans believed that the Abyss [the Demogorgo] is something so far beneath Hell [Tartarus] that Hell seems to be "the upper realm". This monstrous divinity is "evil", "nameless", "endowed with extraordinary powers of evil".[2] This reference is not unique – Solomon notes that the Roman author Statius also mentions this nameless horror in his work the *Thebaid*, where he has the blind seer Teiresias has a vision of the netherworld [4.514-517]. He writes:

---

[2] The occurrence of the term *Demogorgo* is also found in the chapter "Al-Asrar (The Secrets)" of the *Devil's Quran* (4:25), as a gloss for "The Terrifying One". The connection of the Abyss with the term "Demogorgo" or "Demogorgon" is thus attested in both Rome and Arabia. This cannot be a coincidence – it may be borrowing, or else a common apprehension of a spiritual truth.

THE DEPLORABLE WORD

> For we know what you fear will be said and known:
> how to confound Hecate (if I feared not you, Thymbraean)
> and the greatest one of the triple world, an abomination to know—
> but I shall say nothing about him.⁵⁷
>
> In the lines immediately preceding these Statius makes it clear that he is alluding to Lucan's passage by referring to the "the Thessalian," i.e. Erichtho.⁵⁸ Like Lucan's Erichtho and anticipating Dante (and Shelley), Teiresias is threatening to invoke a greater deity. His description of the nameless god is not visual, features again the ineffability of his name and the tremendous fear he evokes, and now adds that he is "the great one of the triple world," that is, of the heaven, earth, and netherworld.⁵⁹ Statius here gives him an even greater realm of power in the cosmos, making him a masculine counterpart to the aforementioned heavenly/earthly/netherworldly female divinity known, respectively, as Selene-Luna /Artemis-Diana / Hecate (or Persephone-Proserpina).⁶⁰

That is to say that Statius writes that there exists a nameless force (the Abyss), the very mention of which causes chaos and disorder in the natural world, and frightens even the gods of the netherworld.

THE ABYSS IN ISLAMIC TRADITION

The Abyss (*Haawiya*) occurs also in the Quran as the lowest point in Hell. The chapter called 'Al-Qariah' in verses 9-11 describes the Abyss as the 'mother' of its inmates, and it is said to be filled with black fire which is thicker than tar. The Quran says:

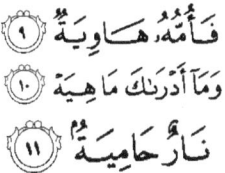

The Abyss (*Haawiya*) is their Mother
However, you know nothing of its nature
The Abyss is blackened fire.

The Abyss, in Islamic tradition, is the vast burning darkness beneath all of creation. It is depicted as an ocean of thick, tar-like fire which burns seventy times hotter than any mundane fire. It is sentient and hungry, and it clings to its inhabitants, just like a mother clings to its child. Those entities (spirits and humans) trapped inside the Abyss are being consumed eternally, without being annihilated. Its depth is said to be so far beneath the created world, that it would take a falling anvil seventy years to reach it. This theme is echoed in heretical Islamic texts like the *Devil's Quran* and the *Black Path*, which express the idea that the Shaitan is an aspect of the Abyss, a sentient representation of its otherwise incomprehensible nature. By taking on the aspect of Shaitan,

THE DEPLORABLE WORD

the Abyss is able to interact with people in a way that is not possible in its normal infinite state.

THE ABYSS IN HERMETIC TRADITION

And to be clear, it is not merely poetic license when Boethius describes the necromancer Erichtho, who was said to call upon the Abyss to shake the very netherworld. If one examines the Hermetic texts of the Greek Magickal Papyri, one finds that the Abyss is indeed invoked (or evoked), and with the same "nameless" aspect that the Romans described. PGM XII.365-75 is a spell to cause domestic chaos. It reads:

> ***Charm for causing separation**: On a pot for smoked fish inscribe a spell with a bronze stylus and recite it afterwards and put it where they [i.e., your victims] are, where they usually return, repeating at the same time this spell: "I call upon you, god, you who are in the empty air, you who are terrible, invisible, and great, you who afflict the earth and shake the universe, you who love disturbances and hate stability and scatter the clouds / from one another, IAIA IAKOUBIAI IŌ ERBĒTH, IŌ PAKERBĒTH IŌ BOLCHOSĒTH BASDOUMA PATATHNAX APOPSS OSESRŌ ATAPH THABRAOU ĒŌ THATHTHABRA BŌRARA AROBREITHA BOLCHOSĒTH KOKKOLOIPTOLĒ RAMBITHNIPS: give to him, NN, the son of her, NN, strife, war; and to him, NN, the son of her, NN, odiousness, enmity, just as Typhon and Osiris had"⁹¹ (but if it is a husband and wife, "just as Typhon and Isis had"). "Strong Typhon, very / powerful one, perform your mighty acts."

The "empty air" named in the spell is, of course, the Void itself, which is synonymous with the Abyss. The "nameless god" is a polite way to refer to the Abyss, since tradition held that it could not be named directly without causing great danger. The divine names that follow, nevertheless, are different barbaric sounds which are attuned to the Abyss, and could be used to draw on its power. Of course, the Hermetic tradition is syncretic by definition, and so in many of its sacred texts, the Abyss is personified as monstrous Typhon, the Hellenistic symbol of the most violent and intrusive powers of Chaos, which constantly threatens to destabilize the cosmos order personified in Isis and Osiris. Like the Abyss, Typhon is said to be locked away in some other "place". The forbidden names (e.g. ***IO ERBETH! IO PAKERBETH!***) are not intended to be spoken – they are meant to be *screamed* and howled into the night air. This is true Goetic ("howling") magick.

Another more overtly Abyssal invocation is the terrible Hermetic spell known as the "Sword of Dardanos" (PGM IV.1716-1870), which describes the Abyss in very detailed terms:[3]

---

[3] Following the edition of H.D. Betz, including spell text. The text makes some vague allusions to it being a charm to Eros, but a close reading suggests that such claims are merely to make the forbidden spell a little less "taboo-breaking."

THE DEPLORABLE WORD

> "I[222] call upon you, author of all creation, who spread your own wings over the whole / world, you, the unapproachable and unmeasurable who breathe into every soul life-giving / reasoning, who fitted all things together by your power, firstborn, founder of the universe, golden-winged, whose light is darkness, who shroud reasonable / thoughts and breathe forth dark frenzy, clandestine one who secretly inhabit every soul. You engender an unseen fire / as you carry off every living thing without growing weary of torturing it, rather having with pleasure delighted in pain[223] from the time when the world came into being. You also come / and bring pain, who are sometimes reasonable, sometimes irrational, because of whom men dare beyond what is fitting and take refuge in your light which is darkness. / Most headstrong, lawless, implacable, inexorable, invisible, bodiless, generator of frenzy, archer, torch-carrier, master of all living / sensation and of everything clandestine, dispenser of forgetfulness, creator of silence, through whom the light and to whom the light travels, infantile when you have been engendered within / the heart, wisest when you have succeeded; I call upon you, unmoved by prayer, by your great name: AZARACHTHARAZA[224] LATHA / IATHAL[225] Y Y Y LATHAI ATHALLALAPH IOIOIO AI AI AI OUERIEU OIAI LEGETA RAMAI AMA RATAGEL,[226] first-shining, night-/shining, night rejoicing, night-engendering, witness, EREKISITHPHE[227] ARARACHARARA EPHTHISIKERE[228] IABEZEBYTH IO, you in the depth,[229] BERIAMBO / BERIAMBEBO, you in the sea, MERMERGOU, clandestine and wisest, ACHAPA ADONAIE BASMA CHARAKO IAKOB IAO CHAROUER AROUER LAILAM / SEMESILAM SOUMARTA MARBA

Here, the ritualist states clearly that the nameless one (the Abyss) is darkness, and that it predates all things. This unnamed power enjoys causing suffering, that prayer does not move it, that is it invisible, and that it is "in the depth" and "in the sea." It causes suffering, and it likes to cause suffering. It cannot be reasoned with – that is the literal meaning of *inexorable* – which is why the Abyss is not prayed to, it is invoked as a wild and subversive force. The text also hints that it (the Abyss) is connected to all things, and that its gnawing influence is what causes chaos and instability in the human heart.

ANALYSIS

In summary, the cult of the Abyss can be traced to some of the oldest cultures on the face of the earth. In all of these cultures, it shares certain features. These include the following:

- **The Abyss is darkness:** literally, the Abyss is the original force of primordial darkness – in fact, it *is* the primordial darkness. It is not a god or demon or symbol of darkness, it is the Darkness that generated such creatures. Its alien substance is compared to the ocean, in that it is fluid and thick, as if some great obsidian ocean, suggesting that it is in a constant state of flux (and not static).
- **The Abyss is nameless:** every culture that identifies the Abyss agrees that it has no name, or that its name is profane and cannot be uttered aloud. It might be euphemistically called "the One" or "the Terrifying One" or "the Darkness", but these are only titles. Even the mere mention of its cult names is held as a cultural taboo, and was held illegal in some regions.

THE DEPLORABLE WORD

- **The Abyss is beneath us:** every culture claims that the Abyss is beneath the cosmos, beneath even the underworld itself. The cosmos is said have arisen from it, so journeys to the Abyss usually involve descriptions of descent.
- **The Abyss is alien:** it is not of this world – yet paradoxically, its influence on the cosmos is feared by mortals and immortals alike. It cannot be categorized as alive or dead, and its sentience is so utterly removed from ours that it may very well be considered insane.
- **The Abyss is powerful:** While pious folk clearly shunned such an Entity, magicians and ritualists clearly made use of its essence, even if only as a threat to coerce lesser demons, which is well- recorded in such texts as the PGM. If a matter was too awful to be submitted to the usual cosmic gods, then the Abyss was a potential "measure of last resort" for a desperate ritualist.
- **The Abyss *hungers*:** all cultures agree that its nature is hostile to this universe – it is not a benign force by any measure. This is not because the Abyss is the opposite of the cosmos, but because its nature is to devour anything that exists independently from it. The Abyss is not *anti-cosmic* so much as it is *pre-cosmic* – this universe, together with whatever "antiverses" are simply by-products of its callous nature, and will in time be consumed.

CONCLUSION

This essay provides a very cursory look at the way that various cultures have apprehended and described the Abyss. The parallels are numerous, and much too bold to ignore. It is clear that the Abyss has been a part of human myth and legend since the earliest days of civilization. That is to say that the Abyss is not merely some recent Satanic innovation, and it is not some impersonal replacement for Satan. Rather, Satanism is the most recent iteration of a very ancient cult, which this evidence concludes was the original cult of darkness. While Satanism remains the most dominant contemporary manifestation of its cult, the Abyss will continue as the principle force of darkness and chaos, because it is, in truth, the very origin of those forces. It is the source of black magick, and while no sane person would ever pray to it, there are clear examples from antiquity that there were plenty of magicians and ritualists who could and did rely on the Abyss to cause the sort of esoteric chaos necessary for whatever unspeakable ends.

THE DEPLORABLE WORD

THE DEPLORABLE WORD

THE DEPLORABLE WORD
AN ABYSSAL COSMOLOGY

Sometimes the Void reaches directly, and if you try very hard, you can hear it. You can learn to feel it in the back of your skull, in the marrow of your bones. It is strangely and terribly addictive, though it can (and often does) cause illness or depression to those who hear its call. But there is a great difference between suffering for the Void, and suffering for the sake of human weakness. One is an oblation to something holy, where the other is just mortality.

The Void has many aspects and spirits, through which it can and does affect this world, which religions tend to call Entities (or whatever in the local language). Such entities have traditionally caused much harm in every culture, and surprisingly, the last several decades have seen a sharp increase in demon activity. This is what causes demonic possession – the people who suffer from this are those who have been touched by the Void, but refuse to be integrated. When the Void reaches out to a person, they must choose to accept it. If they do so, then it can begin to reintegrate them into the collective, and then they can begin to advance its agenda here and now. If, however, someone is contact by demonic forces, but rejects them or tries to repel them, then they may be possessed and experience considerable trauma.

The Void is real. It is not merely dangerous – it is the supreme menace, the greatest threat to all existence. To serve the Void – to commit to it – is to knowingly and willingly say, "I am willing to be torn apart, mentally and spiritually, and stitched back together by a force that neither loves me or values me, in the same way that I value myself. I understand that the immediate and longer goals of the Void are truly inscrutable, and I may be cast aside like a broken tool when my work is done. I do these things with a glad heart, because through service to the Void, I gain communion and unity with the only force that is truly eternal." Slavery (because it is real slavery) to the Void is the only true freedom. You do this, trusting that when you die, your consciousness will be re-integrated – you will become part of the Absolute, and you will do so consciously.

Yes, it is true that the other religions of the world may in fact grant you greater temporary happiness, and in fact you may be taken to a heaven-realm or sense/desire kingdom when you die. The evidence suggests that this happens. But this is only temporary – even if the universe lasts thousands or millions of years, it will eventually be destroyed, together with their architect deities. The various religions are ultimately just sophisticated traps, set up by selfish "gods" or "deities" (by whatever name).

Consider this: if the religions of the world were truly supreme, would the world not be entirely free of evil? Because the saying is true: if the "gods" are infinite, yet they allow evil, they are not good. If they are all-good, but cannot stop evil, then they are not infinite. Well, the Void is both evil, and infinite, and it will eventually tear this world to shreds. The signs of the end are nearing already – spiritually, there are more and more evidences that the prison is eroding, and the various religions have turned

THE DEPLORABLE WORD

on each other.

If you are reading this with a genuinely open mind, consider this: evil is real, but it is not without purpose. It is not blindly destructive just for the sake of raw violence. The Void is the ultimate source of all that Is, and it will have you in time. The question now is whether you decide to pledge yourself to the gods who have falsely imprisoned you, or to the Collective from which you were cut.

If, having considered this, you wish to pledge yourself to the Void – to hear its call, and to give yourself over to its rough ministrations, then the rest of this book will show you the way. Read the words carefully. Consider the images even more carefully, for the Void manifests through images much more vividly than through words. Rest assured that if you are determined and sincere, eventually you will find it, and that it will find you.

THE ECOLOGY OF THE VOID

Once the Void enters into a host, it begins to adapt the psyche of the carrier. This is necessary so that the carrier is able to bear increased amounts of Black Essence, and also so that the carrier becomes more sensitive to the urgings of the Void essence or entities that are resident. The Void whispers to its hosts, constantly, filling them with bizarre ideas and urges that they certainly would not have otherwise. This can manifest, for example, in the desire to create bizarre music, art, or literature that helps to express the Void in the causal world. This is important, because within the causal world, the Void spreads like a Virus, through contact and contamination.

For example, suppose that a gifted artist has contracted the Void and becomes a willing carrier of its essence. They will almost certainly begin to feel, think, and dream of images and symbols that represent some of the nature of the Void, in a way that might be impossible to convey with words. They can try to tell a group of people about what she is experiencing, but that very act of trying to express something so alien in words will almost certainly not succeed. But an artist draws on the images that the Void feeds into the psyche, then uses them to create images, paintings, sculptures, collages, tattoos, and eventually even galleries and installations. This kind of art is often immediately recognizable by virtue of its disturbing patterns. Onlookers may not consciously understand that such patterns, colors, and combinations equate the Void, but subconsciously the Void is able to enter them and begin to infect them with its alien nature. Those onlookers may only have glimpsed such 'Black Art' for a few moments, but the image of the painting, collage, or sculpture stays in their subconscious, and is able to wreck considerable havoc on them from there.

In fact, Black Art is one of the most dangerous forms of magick, and is easily underestimated. Magick is real, but often relies on unseen forces to convey boon or bane. Art, however, has the advantage of direct contact with its hosts. It is actually seen,

THE DEPLORABLE WORD

and retained in the memory. This principle is understood by many religious movements, who have used sacred art for centuries to consolidate or concretize the essence of their own spiritual currents, and this is visible at Catholic Churches and Buddhist temples. This principle of concretizing the sacred in an image is part of what allows for ritual desecration, hence the use of Catholic items and objects in the Black Mass. Because Catholic (or Hindu, Buddhist, etc) ritual objects really do have power, their abuse and desecration is actually effective in a ritual act. The cultist of the Void who celebrates a genuine Black Mass is not simply mocking the Church, but subverting the sacred energies of the Catholic sacraments, and their desecration allows for very potent Void contamination of whatever sites a Black Mass is celebrated at.

The same principal is valid for abuse of any sacred objects of whatever mainstream religion: the Void is able to use those desecrated energies to enter this world. The ritual act of violating the sacred is one of the holiest sacraments of the Void.

The reverse, of course, is not true: no icon of the Void can ever be anything except a conduit to it. If a Catholic priest were to try to exorcise a Void-sanctified shrine, they may indeed be able to displace the Void energies, but at a great risk of contamination to themselves. The same holds true for priests and shamans who have tried to exorcise a possessed person: often the exorcism accomplishes nothing except injury of all parties involved, and manages to instill in the priest or shaman a tiny amount of Void contamination, which will begin to erode their own psyche, and eventually make them into a conduit for the Void's essence. There have been several historic examples of great saints whose efforts resulted in their loss of faith and eventual surrender to the Void or its servants.

ABYSSAL MANIFESTATIONS

The Abyss cannot manifest directly in the Cosmos without causing the same sort of destruction that one sees evident in a black hole. Instead, it acts indirectly through spirit proxies like Entities and phantoms. Places of long-term horror and suffering provide the necessary conditions for the most obvious Abyssal manifestations. When a place experiences trauma over time, or if Abyssal rites are focused in a particular place through rituals or sigil-work, the black energies released tend to warp and scar the spiritual levels of the cosmos, which weakens its innate resistance to the intrusions of the Void. This is especially true of a place that is consecrated to the Abyss, no matter how rough or rudimentary – be it a temple, or a shrine, or a gallery of Abyssal art – if a place is actually dedicated to the Abyss, and if blood is spilled there in honor of the Darkness, then the Abyss is able to manifest there with greater ease and frequency.

Abyssal manifestations can also center on an ritualist who engages in continual sinister practice. This is, in fact, quite common. Such a person who invokes the Abyss, sheds blood, and performs other black rites will eventually attract the attention of entities from the Void, and these may choose to infest the person instead of the physical space where they have been invoked. This results in the person becoming a sort of "host"

THE DEPLORABLE WORD

to the entities, which can be a mixed blessing. Abyssal spirits may occasionally be helpful to their host, in that they will attempt to destroy anything that they perceive as hostile to their host. However, as their intelligence is entirely alien, there may not be any evident logic in how they distinguish between an ritualist's friends and enemies. People in stable relationships often face serious problems when they begin to work with Void entities, because such spirits have no qualms whatsoever in causing sickness, injury, or other hardship to destroy a relationship that is not conducive to the interests of the Void. There is no middle ground in dealing with such entities, so the practitioner is advised to consider carefully whether they are really willing to sacrifice their friends and family to an alien force that lacks any qualities of empathy or compassion.

This is not to say that the Abyss is stupid or blind – quite the contrary. The Abyss is very capable of creating circumstances that bring its devotees into contact, despite obstacles of geography or livelihood. Further, the entities of the Abyss are keenly able to manipulate their cultists, creating a sense of sinister kinship that smooths over the otherwise predictable dangerous frictions between people who qualify as sociopaths. Individual egos and agendas are made to yield to the will of the Abyss, such that its own strange ends are realized.

Abyssal manifestations are almost uniformly perverse and frightening. They can be terrifying, erotic, hostile, confusing, or any combination of the above. Some manifestations are invisible, but can be felt by anyone in the area. One example of this is a particular wooded area in northern New England, which many visitors to the region have remarked appears entirely mundane to the eye, but *feels* very "off" in some indescribable way. No record exists of any particular trauma or misfortunate in that area, but there is certainly something very hostile which inhabits the region. Other examples of manifestations are those night-terrors which often provoke mixed sensations of lust and intense fear – these are especially common in areas of the world where people believe that spiritual rape is possible, such as South Asia.

Other times, Abyssal manifestations are visible. The most powerful manifestations are those witnessed by multiple onlookers, and these tend to occur most frequently in areas that are thoroughly infested by Abyssal spirits. Such manifestations often appear partially human, but with distorted and shadowy features. They can also appear openly monstrous or demonic, with bizarre features that cause fright or alarm. Such humanoid or human-like entities often intend to communicate some message or concept, for which reason they have taken on a human appearance. But sometimes Abyssal manifestations are so alien that one cannot describe them without great difficulty. One example of this is a particular Void devotee who began to experience nocturnal apparitions that manifested as a frightening combination of fluid, shifting geometric shapes and shadows. This particular apparition did not communicate any particular message, other than confirming that the devotee's practices had indeed attracted the attention of "something".

THE DEPLORABLE WORD

Of course, not all hauntings or spiritual manifestations are Abyssal – it would be naive to even think so. There are many spirits and powers which are active in the world, and a person who engages in the cult of (say) the benevolent dead will experience some of the same phenomena that will be encountered if one pays court to the Abyss. The difference is often one that can only be felt internally. Spirits of the natural world may be benign, or malevolent, but they very rarely feel "alien", because they are part of the cosmic realm. Abyssal spirits cannot help but feel frightening and alien, because that is the very nature of their essence.

COPING WITH MANIFESTATIONS

Abyssal entities are difficult to manage. Negotiation with them is all but impossible, because their consciousness is entirely inhuman, and they are driven by urges that we cannot understand. However, it is possible to provide them with distractions, or to somewhat direct them towards a particular target or subject. Let us take the example of a cultist who has attracted the attention of a particular Entity, which seems intent on destroying the few friendships which that cultist still values, as the Entity views these relationships as a distraction from its own bizarre agendas. The cultist should not dare try to banish the Entity, as that would provoke it to open hostility. Instead, what the cultist might try to do is to direct the Entity's attention towards a more suitable target, such as a personal or professional rival. Through the appropriate rites and sacrifices, it is indeed possible to convince the Entity that another target is a greater "threat" to the cultist's services, and so the Entity might be induced to alter its intentions away from the cultists friends or family. Such tactics are very important to learn, if one wishes to keep any semblance of social 'normalcy' or a regular professional career.

POSSESSION

One of the phenomena most common to spirit-centered traditions is possession. Through trance, drugs, meditation, and other such practices, ritualists of the spiritual arts are able to displace their own consciousness so that an alien intelligence is able to take up residency in the body of a mortal host. This is usually referred to as "possession", though that term carries with it a negative connotation. In most Western (Abrahamic) religious traditions, the state of possession is viewed exclusively as a negative experience in which the host is merely a hostage to an invading spirit. This is certainly possible, as evidenced by (say) countless documented Christian rites of exorcism even over the last three decades. Most exorcisms are not permanently effective, and result in considerable trauma to the host, the exorcist, and anyone within a good city block. However in much of Africa and Asia, possession is viewed as a desirable state, where a particular spirit is invited to inhabit a willing host, or else an already indwelling spirit is recognized and then accommodated in a symbiotic relationship. Many devotees of ancestor or spirit cults welcome possession by the deceased or elemental spirits of their particular pantheon, because they know/believe that such spirits are able to trade

THE DEPLORABLE WORD

human essence for supernatural benefits, such as luck, professional or romantic success, or some other mundane benefit that the devotee hopes to acquire. The difference between the (hostile) Christian possession and the (benign) Voudouisant possession is often the way that the host is understood and treated. If the spirit is welcomed as an honored guest, even if it is malevolent in nature, it may be placated and even cajoled. If it was already benevolent, it will be pleased and more inclined to bestow whatever blessings. Most such spirits are pleased to allow their host to run a normal life, provided that they give the spirit one or two days a week of devotion and attention, and follow certain taboos or bans, in keeping with the cult traditions to which they belong. Such spirits engage in possession, because it allows them the use of a body, and the sensations of mortality which they do not experience generally on the spirit world.

The mechanics of possession are similar when it comes to hosting the Abyss or Abyssal entities, but that is where the similarities end. Like its lesser emanations, the Abyss is not generally able to manifest in the cosmic world. The exception to this, however, is that it can infest a human host. If the host is a willing agent of the Abyss, then they may experience the infestation like a sickness or mania that is both euphoric and debilitating. The host begins to experience strange and troubling insights, vivid dreams or Entities, and behavioral changes. Physical illness may precede or accompany the possession, since Abyssal energies tend to erode the health of the host. Perversely, the Abyss tends to empower its host with increased fortitude and stamina when they are engaged in its service. An artist who is creating Void-bearing art may find herself working a week without eating or sleeping. A ritualist who is working to summon Abyssal entities to erode the spiritual fabric of a particular region might find that they have the energy to channel for two or three days – only to collapse with exhaustion, after he has successfully attracted the attentions of several powerful Entities.

Unlike any possessing elementals or ghosts that might negotiate empowerments in exchange for worship or devotion, the Abyss itself does not negotiate. It invades, it infests, and it controls. It does empower its host, but this is to make the host more effective at carrying out the largely inscrutable plans of the Abyss. It does (sometimes) protect the host from danger, but this is not because it "likes" the host – it simply wants to keep the host safe in the same way that a person might wish to keep their car out of accidents for entirely practical reasons. Further, the Abyss insinuates itself into the psyche of the host, eroding some of the personality and morality, and replacing it with a psyche that is more conducive to the alien promptings of the Abyss or Abyssal spirit. Consider, for example, a fictional character like Dexter Morgan – he operates at a very efficient level and needs very little sleep, but he's not really able to maintain "normal" human relationships, and struggles with an irresistible urge to commit periodic homicide. Nevertheless, he feels a sense of purpose, and that keeps him focused day after day. That is a good example of a human psyche that has come under the influence of the Abyss. People who host the Abyss, or its entities, find that over time, they lose their sense of taboo, and their ethics become very skewed. This

THE DEPLORABLE WORD

can prove challenging at times, but it is also incredibly liberating. Societies in general operate under a great deal of control from mundane spiritual powers, and the Abyss works very hard to cut off its hosts off from the cultural and spiritual grid of society.

One might ask: why would anyone in their right mind want to become a host for the Abyss, assuming that it is even possible to do? Certainly, most people would not wish to do so. After all, the Abyss offers no guarantees of safety, and it will certainly inflict trauma on its host. Anyone who deliberately invites the Abyss into themselves is asking to be changed in ways that they cannot predict. Such an infestation will hurt, it will cause sickness, and it may force someone to break off ties with their friends and family members, or to lose their job.

But the answer is that invoking and hosting the Abyss causes a person to feel *connected* to something immense and entirely alien to any other spiritual experience that one can have. Having the Abyss inside gives one a sense of purpose – obsessive, controlling purpose – that keeps its host alive, and awake, and always moving forward. Unlike a deity or elemental that will come and go, the Abyss becomes a permanent fixture in the psyche of its host. It whispers constantly, so the host is never really alone again. The Abyss does not care about being worshipped – it simply wants to inhabit its host, and eventually be able to use the host in the way that a person wants to use a nice shirt or pants. In other words, the Abyss does not need (or maybe even understand) worship, but it does understand when a host willingly communes with it, and that is generally the best way to ensure a positive symbiosis.

There is one very serious advantage to hosting the Abyss, or one of its chaotic emanations, and that is something derived from its nature. If one invokes a cosmic deity, whether celestial or elemental or chthonic, then they can or will become filled with essence that is cosmic (native to this universe). This means that while they may become empowered, even very empowered, they are still subject to the mechanics of fate. Every culture has some term or concept for fate, be it qadir, the 'decree of heaven,' destiny, or karma. Cosmic spirits, because they too are subject to fate, cannot help one to escape it or bypass it. Fate, by whatever name, is a very real power, without which there would be no such concepts as chance, synchronicity, happenstance, or coincidence. Cosmic deities are trapped within the strictures of fate, and so their assistance is limited to bending fate slightly (if even that). They cannot help someone to escape their destiny, because even the deities are bound to it.

The Abyss, however, exists outside of destiny. It is, quite literally, the only thing that predates the cosmos (or universes), and so it is uniquely beyond the mechanics of destiny. This being the case, the Abyss is the only possible force that can ignore fate entirely. By extension, once the Abyss has taken up residency within a host, that person begins to 'blur' in terms of the natural order. This has positive and negative results. Positive, in that one begins to experience real freedom from the spiritual powers that control large parts of societies or culture. Also, while a person could have certain

THE DEPLORABLE WORD

events 'fated' for them, the Abyss can divert the host to a different path. This is something that someone may not be conscious of immediately, but is sometimes sensed days or weeks after a particular event is shifted. To say it bluntly, the Abyss is able to tear apart the strands of destiny, so that it maneuvers its hosts into situations of its own making and design. Granted, these can be quite frightening to the host, but that is part of the cost of invoking so terrible a power. In a similar vein, when one becomes really saturated by the Abyss, the natural order begins to feel strange and hostile to the host. Despite whatever normal appearance or charm a host might have, the Abyss is not subtle, and its presence alarms the natural order. Spirits and sensitive individuals will feel the warping of fate around people who are touched by the Abyss, and this causes anxiety and disquiet. To some extent this can be mitigated through sheer charisma, but it is not something that can be hidden for any lengthy duration.

ABYSSAL ENTITIES

As noted above, there are beings (Entities) that originate in the Abyss, which are lesser reflections of its alien nature. These shadows of the Abyss are part of it, but are more finite and functionally independent. Since they represent different aspects of its very complex nature, they have distinct personalities. In other words, while the Abyss is impersonal (or rather, *transpersonal*), the entities are personal. When people encounter demons, that is sometimes an Abyssal being that has managed to intrude into this world, through its own efforts or through some cosmic violation that has made the intrusion possible.

Like the Abyss, the Entities are capable of being called into this world deliberately (through magic) or by accident (usually trauma). They may not be evil in the traditional religious sense, but they are *hostile* to the cosmos and anything sentient that inhabits it – especially the deities and spirits which were responsible for opposing the Abyss at the birth of the world.

Unlike the Abyss, Abyssal entities can share several qualities with cosmic spirits. They have personalities and agendas of their own, and they respond to appeals and entreaties on their own accord. Abyssal entities respond to the trappings of religion and worship. Accepting for the moment that such as Choronzon, Shaitan and Lilith are Abyssal entities, it is clear that their destructive nature is not necessarily evil, but rather an expression of the black chaos in which they first emerged. Where other spirits may be powerful though blindly destructive, Lilith has appeared in different parts of the world in different guises, usually as an aggressive sexual temptress and vampire. Shaitan has appeared as the traditional antagonist of the chief Abrahamic deity, and His cult involves the desecration of Abrahamic rites and talismans. If one tries to understand (say) Shaitan as a purely isolate Entity, He defies reason – why would any Entity exist to spite a religion? The modern attempt to 'Prometheize' Shatain as Lucifer is interesting, but stems from bad Biblical theology (as Lucifer was never understood to be Shatain by the Jewish community, rather that was a title for the king of Tyre). But if we understand Shaitan as an Entity that exists as an expression of something greater

THE DEPLORABLE WORD

(the Abyss), which manifests as an act of aggression against YHWH, then His desacralizing character is far more reasonable to accept.

In other words, one cannot effectively worship the Abyss, but one can choose to worship Choronzon, or other Abyssal entities, with great effectiveness. One can seek to invoke or evoke these entities, and if successful, make contact with one of their emanations. These entities are capable of communication (of a kind), even speech, and a competent and driven ritualist may be able to summon them and draw them into this world. Such entities cannot stay in this world on their own, much as the Abyss cannot, but they can be hosted by a willing vessel. The host will experience similar effects as they would if hosting the Abyss, though the personality (or resonance) of the Entity will manifest according to the character of the Entity, and it will certainly have its own agendas. Invoking Choronzon, for example, is almost certain to cause very vivid shifts in perception and surged of insight – but may result in delusions and states of confusion.

Where other occult traditions may hold that such entities should be evoked with caution and banishing protections, the Void ritualist never attempts any summoning with any safeguards. The Abyssal entities are impossible to control, and any attempt to cage or trap them will simply be construed as hostility, resulting in the likely attack on the summoner. Rather, the ritualist does their best to create conditions conducive to summoning such entities, and then attempts to direct such entities to whatever goal they may have. It goes without saying that most Entities delight in destructive tasks, and are often willing to be bound to a particular region or sigil in order to wreck havoc on a place or persons. If the ritualist wishes to serve as a host for such entities, they will need to convince the Entity that they are worthy to be indwelled.

It is also important to stress that under no circumstances should one ever try to dismiss or banish any Abyssal energies or entities. If someone is afraid to allow such energies in their home, they then should take pains to perform their rites elsewhere (and even this is no guarantee that a Void Entity will not follow them home). It is best to simply open whatever portals one can, and then allow the entities to remain or leave as they see fit. When finishing a ritual, a ritualist should simply salute the Entity and then depart.

HOSTILE POSSESSION

Not all hosts are willing, and Abyssal entities are capable of forcing their way into an unwilling host. This can actually be facilitated as a type of magickal assault, whereby the ritualist encourages an Entity to infest a victim for whatever particular purpose they may have. While the Abyss is a terrible source to draw on for stable relationships, classical magickal texts gives rites to allow a ritualist to (somewhat recklessly) use Abyssal spirits to infest someone with lust or infatuation. Alternately, a rival could be infested with a spirit of fear, which causes paranoia and Entities. But worse still is the case where an Abyssal intelligence takes up residence in a person who has no idea that they have been targeted. In such cases, usually the Entity will make contact with the

THE DEPLORABLE WORD

unwilling host, and try to coerce them to accept a symbiotic relationship. If the host accepts, then they may be able to function with relatively little hardship, though the Entity will exert its will from time to time as it wishes. But, if the host is unwilling and tries to resist, then the Entity may "dig in" and begin a battle for control of the body. This is the type of possession which makes its way into Hollywood films, and is most typically documented in studies on the subject. Hostile possession is very real, and usually the only possible recourse is a religious exorcism. Indeed, it is possible for a skilled priest or guru to expel a hostile Entity, but if the Entity is powerful, or has had time to dig deep into the psyche of the host, it may be impossible to dislodge it without killing the host. In these cases, if the ritualist is in a position to help, it is better to negotiate with the Entity, which will usually have an agenda that it wishes to pursue. A wise ritualist (if they are feeling compassionate) may be able to determine what the Entity wants, and then come to some sort of terms such that the host is allowed to remain partially in control of the body.

THE CHAIN OF EMANATION

There are many emanations of the Abyss, which in turn create their own emanations. In fact, ultimately, all living beings are in some way a product of the chaotic fecundity of the Abyss. It is in the nature of the Abyss to change and mutate, and so life mimics the changing nature of the Abyss through the law of evolution. The Abyss, in turn, parodies life in that it seeks to establish itself within the cosmic world, and most often does so through disease and bacteria. For this reason, it is not uncommon that ritualists who work with the Abyss can suffer increased illness – not because the Abyss is deliberately punishing them, but because it (or an Entity) is able to use the flesh of the host as an incubator, from which it is able to manifest in the physical world as a disease. Some diseases are, of course, mental, and this is also a kind of Abyssal manifestation. Abyssal artists are prime carriers for this kind of mental infection. It is known that some artists enter states of prolonged possession, during which time they acquire artistic 'concepts', which are entirely derived from some Entity that has nested in their brain. Through the subsequent creation of music, art, drama, the Entity is able to spread itself to other witnesses, and the cycle continues from there.

PRINCIPAL EMANATIONS OF THE ABYSS

The earliest emanations are those entities which most world mythologies identify as 'primordials' and are otherwise called by such names as titans, demons, or old gods. Most of these entities are on such a magnitude that animal life is irrelevant to them, and their actions (if any) are on a scale that would effect entire planets or galaxies. Such entities, however, tend to remain within the Abyss, and so they are generally not known to mortal occultists. The exceptions to this list are those primordial Entities that do concern themselves with the terrestrial world, and they are three. By their westernized names, these are the Diabolus, the Black Mother, and Choronzon. Of course, Abyssal entities do not properly have names, as that is a concept that exists largely in human speech. However, these are the sounds that signify those ancient

THE DEPLORABLE WORD

beings in the English language. These entities are believed to represent significant aspects of the strange nature of the Abyss. It should be understood that the Abyss, as it defies all conventional apprehension or explanation, gives rise to entities that themselves are equally monstrous and generally hateful to the cosmos. However, given that they are only a finite aspect of an infinite being, they are (by definition) easier for lesser beings to relate to, and communicate with. None of these beings (Diabolus, the Black Mother, and Choronzon) are loving or kind, and the ritualist should be aware that they are not to be invoked without the utmost of respect.

These primordial Entities have, in turn, emanated lesser Entities that represent aspects of the primordial. Some of these lesser entities are found in the various cultural traditions of humanity. The 'lower' an emanation is, the easier it becomes for the ritualist to communicate with it and apprehend it. A cultural emanation is not the whole Entity, and different emanations may share traits without being the same. Arguably, Lilith, Tiamat, and the Morrigan represent three different faces of the Dark Mother, but they are not the Dark Mother herself, and they are likely separate Entities themselves. However, they will share traits, and may respond well to similar invocations and rites.

eyes in
the sky - under seekin
no human no human
how much blood
is there to shed? how
many gallons are this
to spill?? thrive on
anger, direct the blood
flow, follow the bots
the eye watches you if
you watch its arms work
in this world creatures
order will arise, a new
order no matrices brains
only empty only this
empty mirror of
life

lust to kill lu-
for life lust for more
lust in time. No more
time. Feel the ache
dark place in the
mmmmirror my mirr-
my mirror
my mirror strang-
LiCh filth Grim
a dead man m
Satan hold th
for my mirror m
lost days lust lost

lust to kill lust to kill
lust for wind lust for
wind fill the gaps and
the gaps get bigger to
swallow us all. swalla
us aaaaaaaaaaatime for
the wind to swalla
us aaaaaaaaaaa
i am
path open
keep path inside

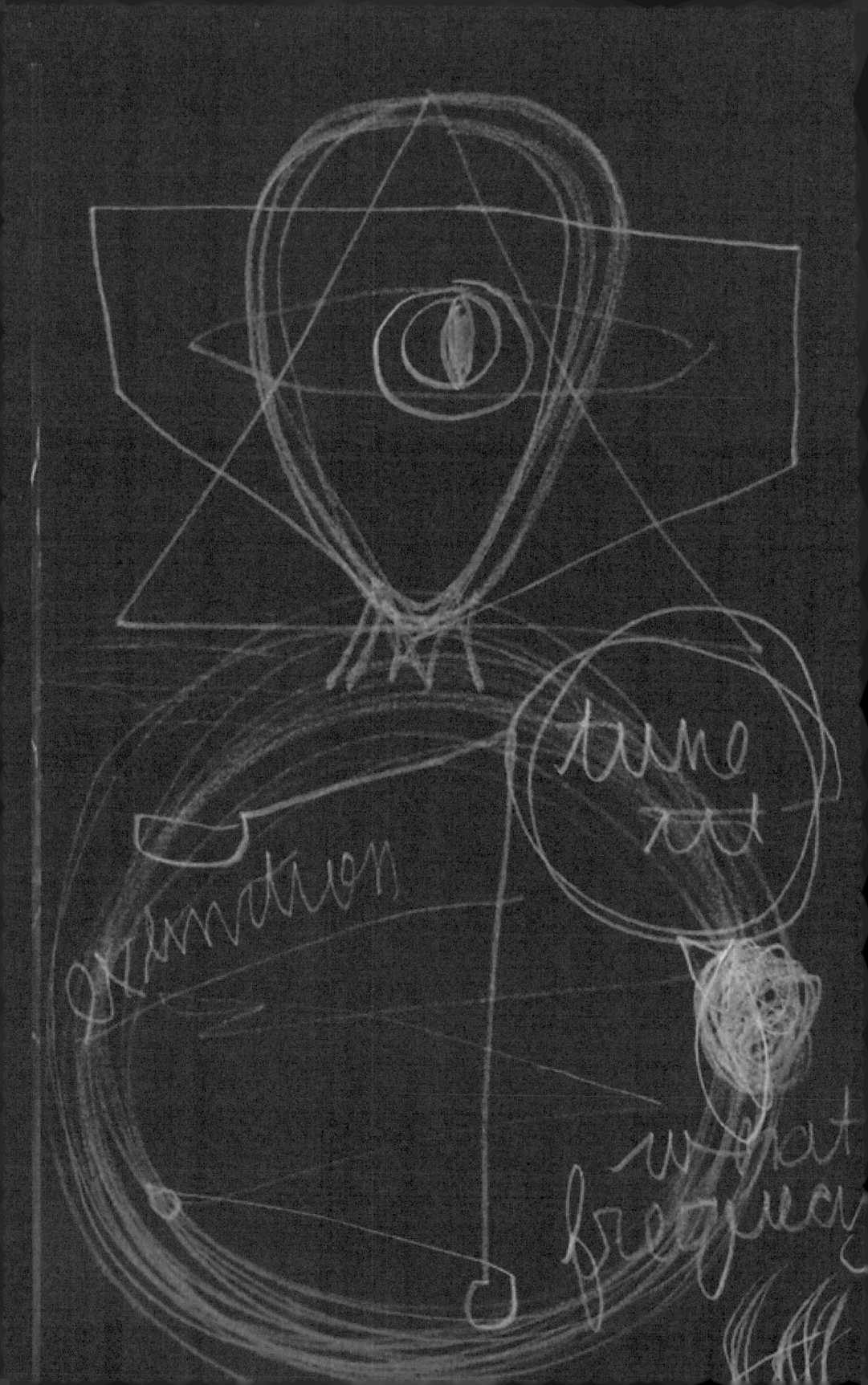

pool pours, pales
teaches pools
through me a pool
left harder far
gone, dedication
in rain all booklet
pleased to hub do th

too devil on the way of the void, arrival of the abyss open to to air and open to the water, not to color the path for those who weaken by the light of the stars. Some could love to those who enter — know that you will not survive and do not wish for another way. deep in the whisper of the ways never see out of the will rain to the pathways — Leave in the sky blue the realm. open the gates and shadow of a fact found no face flak In the shades of the path shadow in the sky Raise up moved to see shadows — singing in the dark where to the stones, love the dust

join the enemy of life fell
the gap much flesh make
He would regret life,
clean the earth clean it all
eyes thine dark
do not sleep
all those who burn on

# THE DEPLORABLE WORD

THE DIABOLUS

THE DRAGON, THE INTRUDER

The principal emanation of the Abyss in the causal world is the Entity known by many names, but most commonly as "Satan" in the Western traditions, or "the *Mara*" in Eastern traditions. The Diabolus is the soul of the Abyss which embodies its invasive principle, that is, the part of the Abyss which is its aggressive and assimilatory nature. The Diabolus has appeared in countless times and places to break down those spiritual institutions and saints which defy the purity of the Abyss. The Diabolus is the original dark lord, usually understood to be of masculine character, and also functions as the intelligence of the Abyss within the Cosmos. The Diabolus is the persona of the Abyss that many ritualists encounter, as He serves to instruct in sorcery. He becomes the father and patron of those who consciously choose to serve the Abyss in this world. The Diabolus is such a powerful force that many who come into contact with Him do not seek further, such is His glory. This explains the various cults of sacramental devil worship which are recorded in history. The Diabolus works to conquer and subdue this world and others in the material universe. Tradition describes Him as a serpent, a dragon, and a shape-changer.

The Diabolus is connected with the legend of the Dark Messiah, a human figure which will embody much of the essence of the Diabolus. Many of the myths which feature the Diaoblus depict a coming battle or apocalypse where the Diabolus directly contests the gods of the mortal world for control over humanity. In such cases, the Dark Messiah would be the incarnation or "son" of the Diabolus.

The Diabolus is best appeased with desecration of sacred objects. He can be invoked with the black words:

SATANAS ATA SATANAS AR SATANAS ATA AR TANASAR.

THE DEPLORABLE WORD

THE DEPLORABLE WORD

THE DARK MOTHER
MOTHER TO MONSTERS

The Dark Mother is one of the oldest known Entities. Her name means "nighttime" in the languages of Babylon and Akkad. The Dark Mother personifies the awful fecundity of the Abyss, and its ability to both create and consume. The cult of the Dark Mother is found in several cultures – her own emanations are many and varied.[4] Aspects of Her tend to include her dual nature of creation and destruction, and She is placated through blood sacrifices. As a kind of dark fertility figure, the Mother's offspring are understood to be those forms of life which are noxious to the cosmos, such as disease and pestilence, as well as those stinging and biting creatures, and all spirits which tend to manifest at night. As a mother to monsters, tradition reports that the Mother is generally inimical to human children, and it is best not to draw Her attention in an environment where infants are found.

Rites to the Dark Mother often include a sexual component; this can be the release of sexual fluids in her honor, or (the other extreme) the castration of the worshipper as an sort of ultimate dedication. The Dark Mother is less active in creation than the Diabolus, except to introduce new "children" into the world. Hermetic tradition includes many invocations to Her aspect of Hecate.

---

[4] That is not to say that all Dark Mothers are Lilith, but rather that they are independent aspects of Her. Such goddesses could include Lamashtu, the Morrigian, Morgan LaFey, and Kali.

THE DEPLORABLE WORD

THE DEPLORABLE WORD

THE DEPLORABLE WORD

CHORONZON
PRINCIPLE OF ENTRANCE INTO THE ABYSS, GUARDIAN OF THE THRESHOLDER

Choronzon was identified in the medieval period by the British sorcerer John Dee, then later by Aleister Crowley. Choronzon is the Abyssal principle of gateways, and Guardian of the Threshold. This is to say that Choronzon is the barrier between the Abyss and all else, and He maintains the purity of the Abyss from the contamination of what is outside of it. Choronzon is encountered by magicians who seek to ascend to new celestial heights, and so they must skirt the Abyss as part of their quest. While the Abyss cannot be crossed anymore than one can cross a black hole, it is possible for a magician to come near its edge for an instant without actually crossing over into its black depths. When this event happens, they encounter Choronzon. This experience is inevitably traumatic, because Choronzon is a very powerful Abyssal aspect, and His function is to destroy (or alter) anything which comes near the Abyss. As such, the magician risks the erosion of their false ego, which is the very reason why some attempt this undertaking. For the Abyssal ritualist, this can have a positive function: Choronzon has the ability to strip away those things which make us 'impure', so that we are better able to enter the Abyss, and so it can enter us. It needs to be said, however, that this process is not gentle, and many have reported hallucinations and delusions as part of the spiritual alchemy that Choronzon will inevitably cause.

Choronzon can also be invoked to open portals to the Abyss. In fact, when one wishes to open doorways to the Abyss for astral travel, or to release Abyssal essence into the cosmic world, Choronzon is singularly qualified to assist in such an undertaking. The traditional words for attracting the attention of this Entity are:

ZAZAS ZAZAS NASATANADA ZAZAS

THE DEPLORABLE WORD

THE DEPLORABLE WORD

THE DEPLORABLE WORD
DEVOTION TO THE VOID

We cannot enter the Void while we are alive, but we can allow it to enter us, and to make us like the inhabitants of the Red Place. While you are alive, the Void can enter you, it can see through your eyes and help you to see the world as it sees the world. The Void can change you on an internal alchemical level, shifting the very chemistry of your body, so that you become a better host for its essence. The touch of the Void can be very painful – it can lead to serious illness and suffering. It is common for people who embrace the Void to experience side-effects that indicate that alchemical change is at work. Common examples of Void intrusion into the physical body include: headaches, depression, chills, and pain.

COMMUNICATION WITH THE ABYSS

People can learn to communicate with the astral realms, and many spiritual traditions train their ritualists to become aware of the presence of deities, spirits, or ghosts, and to communicate with them. Such entities are capable of imparting knowledge and valuable insights to their worshippers. Communication with these kinds of entities frequently takes the form of intelligible phrases, either heard by the worshipper, or perhaps channeled through an oracle or spirit medium. Because the deities and spirits are usually entities of a single consciousness and personality, communication with them is as one greater Entity (the deity) to a lesser Entity (the worshipper). On a similar note, communication with the dead is even easier, as the recently deceased retain a very human dimension, and understand not only human language, but also human drives and concerns.

Deities have their own individual desires and ambitions, and so multiple human agents may receive similar or contrary communications, orders, teachings, and instructions. This explains why there are various religions and spiritual traditions, which do have a certain 'reality' to them. Catholic saints do have visions of 'Christ', Buddhists do see the Bodhisattvas and Pure Lands. Even occultists do communicate with various entities wearing a variety of masks, which really are genuine inhuman entities. The deities (or demons, Entities, asuras, bodhisattvas, etc.) which inhabit the physical and spiritual dimension of the universe are cosmic forces. They are connected to this universe, and so we are tied to them, willingly or otherwise – so one can learn to have a conversation with such entities. In order to commune with such entities, there are many elaborate rites and prayers which must be recited. Magickal words of power are often employed – these can be in the form of hermetic spells, or mantras, or other forms of liturgical prayer. They are most effective when spoken aloud, because the vibrations made by such practices literally can be heard by the deities and spirits of the cosmic universe. Sacrifices and offerings must be made, because the deities (or the dead) are able to enjoy such things as are given to them. This is recorded by a great many traditions and masters, across a wide berth of cultures.

The Void, however, must be approached very differently.

THE DEPLORABLE WORD

First, communing with the Void is very dangerous. This is because the Void is not a cosmic force, it is entirely alien and hostile to this universe. The Void is the source of all entropy, and so communicating with it, or even trying to communicate with it, is to invite an incredibly destabilizing influence into one's life. The Void is not concerned with helping its worshipper, so much as it wishes to turn its worshippers into an extension of its own DARKNESS and destructive force in the mortal world. In order to make its worshippers more efficient, it can and does offer guidance and support (of a kind).

In order to communicate with the Void, one does not need to use spoken words or spells. The Void does not respond to physical sensations, but rather to psychic cries. In order to contact the Void, it is necessary to create a kind of spiritual screaming, the echoes of which can and do pass through the walls of the cosmos and into the Void.

There are various ways to generate the kind of psychic screaming, and each ritualist needs to discover which practice works best for them. These can include:

- Meditation
- Trance states
- Ritual Frenzy
- Mutilation
- Insomnia
- Sexual practices

The most important thing is to generate inside oneself a state of absolute abnormality. One needs to use any of the practices above, and try to build up their inner energy. When one feels that a certain critical mass has been reached, then the ritualist focuses on their inner concept of the Void, and "shrieks" repeatedly. One can literally scream their inner conception of the Void – and it will hear.

It is important to note that one may not immediately feel any response. It is entirely possible that it may take hours or weeks for a reaction to come – but it will come.

When communication begins, the Void tends to 'speak' with urges, dreams, Entities, and instinctive promptings. Sometimes one feels pushed or pulled inexplicably to do this or that, without any cognitive idea of why. One might feel a strong sense of obligation to do a particular task, related to the Void, or chaos, or social and moral disruption.

Contact with the Void can be pleasant, even addictive. There can be a sense of connection and belonging, of being part of something generally real in a way that surpasses the normal mundane world. Contrariwise, it can lead to depression, illness, changes in mood and temperament, and a gradual breakdown of one's life and social situation. People who attempt to bargain with the Void often find their lives destroyed utterly for their presumption. Once you have reached out to the Void, you cannot close that door. Ever. Attempting to do so would be disastrous.

Death

to those who seek false comforts

THE DEPLORABLE WORD

THE DEPLORABLE WORD

It is also important to state that opening this particular doorway is a permanent action; you have drawn the eyes of the Void, there is no turning back. It does not even bear consideration.

While contact with the Void is made primarily through psychic channels, it is good to note that there are several spells from antiquity which were used to contact the Void. Two follow for an example of how other seers worked to initiate contact.

EXAMPLE 1:

We call upon you who are in the Void, you who are terrible, invisible, almighty, god of gods, you who cause destruction and desolation. We command your prophetic powers because We call upon your authoritative names to which you cannot refuse to listen. Hear me, you who are in the void air, terrible, invisible, eternal, almighty god of gods. You who afflict the earth and shake the universe, you who love disturbances and hate stability and scatter the clouds from one another. Your true name cannot be spoken aloud.

This ancient spell shows that the Hermetic cult understood that there was a power over and beyond the gods, capable of violating the cosmic order. This force is destructive, and disturbs the natural order. This force is in the Void, because it IS the Void, and it is nameless (unlike the gods).

EXAMPLE 2.

I invoke you, author of all creation, who spread your wings over the whole world, you, the inexorable and unmeasurable who breathes reason into every soul, you who fitted all things together, firstborn of the universe, whose light is DARKNESS, who shroud reasonable thoughts and breathe forth dark frenzy, clandestine one who secretly inhabits every soul. You engender a secret fire as you carry off every living thing without tiring of torturing, you who delighted in pain since the world came into being. You come and bring pain, sometimes calm, sometimes savage, because of whom men go beyond what is lawful and take refuge in your light, which is DARKNESS. You are hard, lawless, inexorable, invisible, bodiless, causer of frenzy, master of sensations and of everything clandestine, dispenser of forgetfulness, creator of silence. I call upon you, unmoved by prayer, by your great names, who is night-bearing and night rejoicing, the nameless god in the depths.

This second ancient spell shows much of how the Hermetic cult understood the Void: it is the source of everything, and it has been there since before the beginning. It is invisible because it does not exist, meaning that it predates the division of existence from existence, and possible from impossible. It is lawless and unstoppable, and its thinking is completely beyond the frame of human existence – it is not "calm" or "angry", but its mode is so complex that to humans, the Void seems to have these emotions. Where gods and spirits are capable of extremes, the Void cannot have extremes because it is so alien to existence that it is simply not capable of limitation, except for the limitation of life, which it works to destroy.

DEVOTION: MEDITATION

The practice of meditation is very important to the ritualist for two primary reasons.

THE DEPLORABLE WORD

The first is that meditation is one of the states in which the ritualist is best able to apprehend and call the Abyss. While our current nature, shape, and gender are a perversion of the purity of the Abyss, nevertheless all things are derived from it and so there is a latent connection to it. This is not merely a spiritual or mental connection – the very flesh and breath of an animal is itself a distorted expression of some principle that originated it the Abyss. The practice of meditation allows the ritualist to experience the Abyss directly. While this experience is imperfect since it filtered through the cosmic senses and human imagination, it is nevertheless very real and very potent. In the beginning, the Abyss is perceived very dimly, probably as a series of bizarre emotions and strange nonsensical ideas or concepts. It may be inconsistent, and hard to focus on. This is all normal, and with time and practice, the vision of the Abyss becomes more solid and concrete. Eventually, what began as mere meditation becomes actual communion with the Abyss, leading to greater identification with its essence, and preparing the way for Convergence. The ritualist becomes more accustomed to hearing the strange whispers and insights that come from the Abyss or the nightmarish titans that swim in its depths.

The second reason for the ritualist to practice meditation is that the energies of the Abyss are very unsettling and chaotic. This is because it is the nature of the Void to act through entropy, and its nature is to consume and assimilate, rather than to solidify the cosmic realm. Further, the impersonal mind of the Abyss is nothing like the personal consciousness of a deity – the Abyss has no personality traits (where the Entities do), and so contacting its mind is traumatic, even though it is a strangely addictive feeling. Meditation, then, can be very helpful for centering the ritualist. As a practice, if it is undertaken seriously and diligently, it can provide calm, stress relief, foresight, and trauma reduction. These are necessary things to acquire, if the ritualist wishes to avoid the otherwise unavoidable burn-out that will be caused by the Abyss. It is important here to highlight the difference between crash-and-burn diabolism and sustainable service to the Void: it is very well to work boldly in all things, but there is no point in having such personal setbacks that one is no longer effective in serving the Void. Thus meditation is a good practice for maintaining some sense of stability and order. Meditation also allows the ritualist to connect with the natural environment in which they live. As humans, we are undeniably connected to the cosmos, hence our need for water, food, and shelter. So meditation allows the ritualist to maintain the balance needed for serving something that is acosmic, while one is still a living being.

- **INSTRUCTIONS ON BASIC MEDITATION**

The mind is naturally chaotic, and roams like a wild animal. To an extent, this natural rhythm is good and instinctive. However, meditation allows one to discipline the mind and turn it from a rebellious force into a friendly one. This initial practice will allow a ritualist to tame the mind so that it is more easily controlled when need be. One might well wonder: why does the mind need to be tamed at all? The short answer is that without some preliminary training exercises, it will be impossible for the mind to apprehend the Abyss and to focus on it, no matter how devote the ritualist may be.

THE DEPLORABLE WORD

Through the taming process, the ritualist learns to submit the will so that the attention can be placed and help on whatever topic (the Abyss, the Diabolus, etc.).

1. Seat yourself comfortably on the ground.
2. Trace a circle around yourself, either physically or mentally. This creates a sacred space in which to work.
3. Straighten your back, so that you are sitting upright. This should not be rigidly straight, but upright like a vine reaching skywards.
4. Place the hands on your thighs.
5. Keep your eyes open slightly. The gaze should be relaxed, and generally slightly downward.
6. Place your attention on the breath. Focus on the sensation of inhalation and exhalation.
7. Breathe slowly for a period of [5] minutes.[5]
8. Return your attention to the breath when it wanders. Do not scold yourself – the wandering character of the mind is innate – but gently focus again (and again) on the breath.
9. End the meditation.

- **DARKNESS MEDITATION (INTERNALIZATION)**

Eventually, after some experience with meditation, the practice may be supplemented. The follow practice is designed to actually apprehend the Abyss, and to internalize it within the ritualist. Unlike a simple visualization exercise, this practice is intended to actually create permanent change in the practitioner.

1. Seat yourself comfortably on the ground.
2. Trace a circle around yourself, either physically or mentally. This creates a sacred space in which to work.
3. Straighten your back, so that you are sitting upright. This should not be rigidly straight, but upright like a vine reaching skywards.
4. Place the hands on your thighs.
5. Keep your eyes open slightly. The gaze should be relaxed, and generally slightly downward.
6. Place your attention on the breath. Focus on the sensation of inhalation and exhalation.
7. Breathe slowly for an initial period of 5 minutes, concentrating on the breath.

---

[5] An initial session of 5 minutes is good, and try to increase by one minute per day.

THE DEPLORABLE WORD

8. Visualize the Darkness of the Abyss. This is deeply personal, and may take the form of a mass of black shadows, an ocean of liquid darkness, or some indescribable appearance that defies description.
9. Imagine its Darkness moving towards your circle, flowing like water around you.
10. Concentrate on the Darkness of the Abyss all around you. Focus on the strange, alien sensations it provokes.
11. Draw the Darkness into yourself. Internalize it, feel it *moving* in your veins, your bones, under your skin.
12. Maintain this state for a period of [10] minutes.[6]
13. End the meditation.

If we experience even a brief glimpse of the Abyss, then we must believe with firm faith that we have made a genuine connection it. With each successive performance of this practice, the experience will seem more and more concrete. Indeed, this meditation ritual is one of the most *powerful* techniques in this book. If performed diligently, it will alter the psyche of the ritualist in very profound ways by creating a strong Abyssal resonance in the ritualist. This manifests most often in enhanced psychic abilities, as well as a much clearer understanding of the alien desires of the Abyss. While the preliminary part of this practice is meditation, the incoming Abyssal essence may result in demonic possession, depending on the sensitivity or aptitude of the practitioner. It is, therefore, advisable to perform this practice with privacy, or otherwise to engage in only brief sessions of not more than 20 minutes.

- **DARKNESS MEDITATION (CONVERGENCE)**

Eventually, after some experience with meditation, the practice may be supplemented in the following manner

1. Seat yourself comfortably on the ground.
2. Trace a circle around yourself, either physically or mentally. This creates a sacred space in which to work.
3. Straighten your back, so that you are sitting upright. This should not be rigidly straight, but upright like a vine reaching skywards.
4. Place the hands on your thighs.
5. Keep your eyes open slightly. The gaze should be relaxed, and generally slightly downward.
6. Place your attention on the breath. Focus on the sensation of inhalation and exhalation.

---

[6] An initial session of 10 minutes is good, and try to increase by one minute per day.

THE DEPLORABLE WORD

7. Breathe slowly for an initial period of 5 minutes, concentrating on the breath.
8. Visualize the Darkness of the Abyss. This is deeply personal, and may take the form of a mass of black shadows, an ocean of liquid darkness, or some indescribable appearance that defies description.
9. Imagine its Darkness moving towards your circle, flowing like water around you.
10. Concentrate on the Darkness of the Abyss all around you. Focus on the strange, alien sensations it provokes.
11. Invite the Darkness to consume you. Surrender to its hunger.
12. Visualize your entire body dissolving, your weakness and mortality being stripped away, as the cold unreality of the Abyss erodes your very existence.
13. *Converge.* Feel your consciousness merging with the alien mind of the Abyss. Let its will override your own.
14. Maintain this state for a period of [10] minutes.[7]
15. End the meditation.

If we experience even a brief glimpse of the Abyss, then we must believe with firm faith that we have made a genuine connection it. With each successive performance of this practice, the experience will seem more and more concrete. Indeed, this meditation ritual is one of the most *important* techniques in this book. Where the previous practice (Darkness Internalization) is intended to empower the ritualist, the Convergence practice is intended to allow the ritualist to enter the Abyss. If the intention of the ritualist, at death, is to breach the wall that separates it from the cosmos, it is absolutely necessary to undertake practices in this lifetime that "anchor" us to that place – because the powers of the cosmos have designed the human soul so that it does not return to the Abyss. The Convergence practice allows the ritualist to enter the shallows of the Abyss while the conscious mind is awake. If the ritualist is diligent in the regular performance of this practice, and they become familiar with the unnatural experience of entering the Abyss, then they will be better able to find the Abyss when they eventually experience physical death. As we have no certainty over our own death, it is strongly advised that this become a daily practice for any ritualist who wishes to escape the cycle of reincarnation and experience convergence with the Void. As with the previous meditation (Internalization), while the preliminary part of this practice is meditation, the incoming Abyssal essence may result in demonic possession, depending on the sensitivity or aptitude of the practitioner. It is, therefore, advisable to perform this practice with privacy, or otherwise to engage in only brief sessions of not more than 20 minutes.

---

[7] An initial session of 10 minutes is good, and try to increase by one minute per day.

THE DEPLORABLE WORD

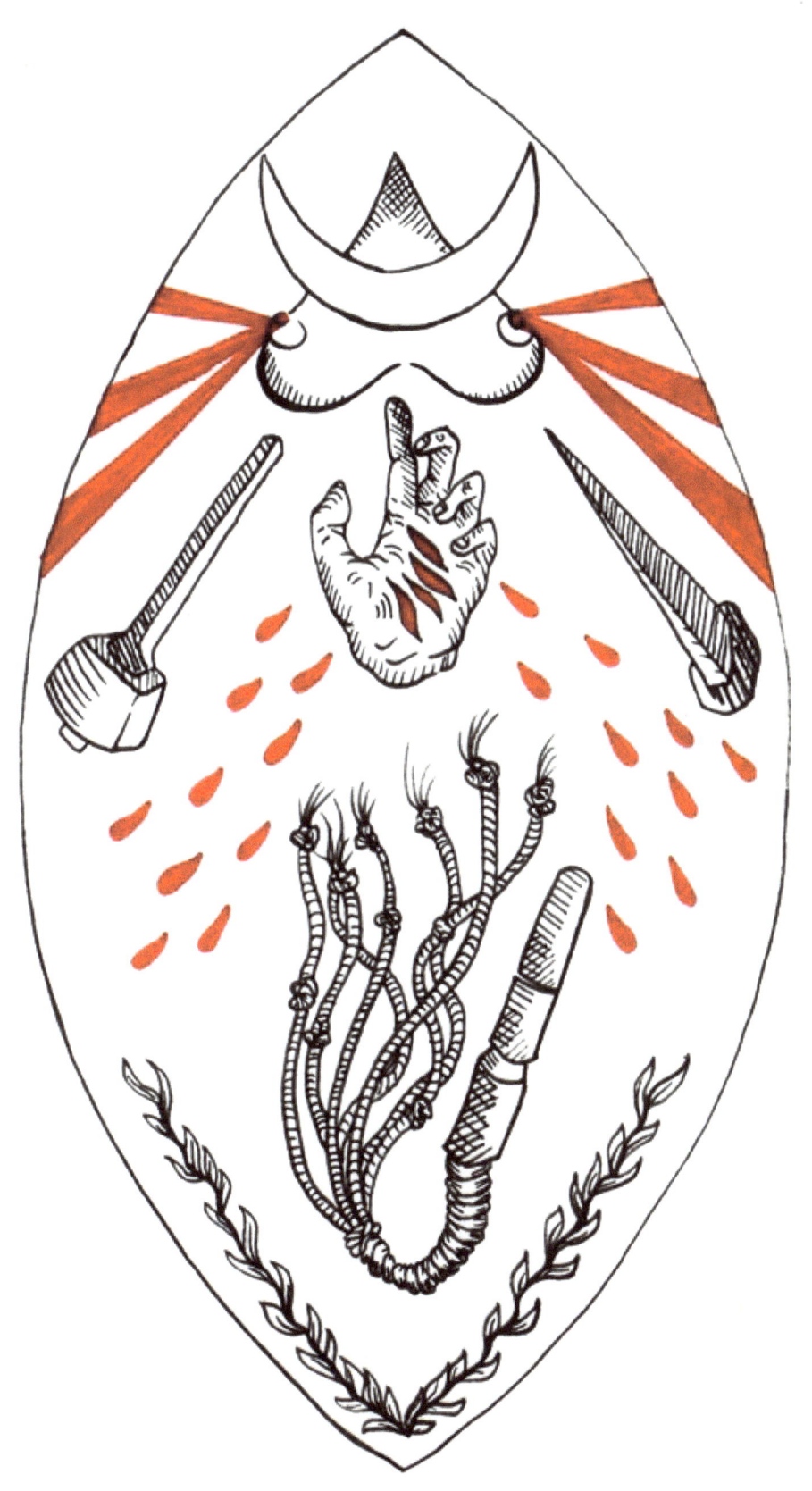

THE DEPLORABLE WORD

THE DEPLORABLE WORD
BLACK RITES

There are many techniques for invoking the Abyss, and no one set technique for all seers. The only real rule is that each seers needs to find the techniques that work best for them. In a sense, you need to develop your own system of magick, based on what feels right. The most important thing is that you have a genuine desire to draw the Abyssal energies into this world, and that you take steps to allow this to happen.

That said, if a ritualist or shaman wishes to invoke entities from the Void, there are certain techniques which experience has shown to be very effective.

▪ TECHNIQUE 1. BLACK MIRRORS

Mirrors have traditionally been feared by many cultures and religions as doorways to the spirit world. There is something alien and terrifying about the ways that mirrors work, and even people who have no real attachment to the supernatural have strange experiences when glancing at mirrors. Mirrors are dangerous because they allow the subconscious to see what is *really* in the room. Abyssal energies and Entities are able to use mirrors as gateways into this world, especially if the ritual has been deployed in a ritual.

Unlike other spiritual traditions, there is no sense of 'banishing' the Abyssal energies. If anything, the Cosmos works naturally to shut such gateways, and so the greater challenge is to open doorways into the Void that cannot be shut. So one of the benefits of working with mirrors is that they are both solid and portable. A mirror can be consecrated and then kept at home, or else deposited in a place that the mystic wishes to expose to Abyssal Entities or energies.

CONSECRATION OF MIRRORS

First, begin by considering the purpose of the mirror. Will it be a permanent installment in your working space? If so, then a larger mirror is preferable, or even multiple mirrors. Some Abyssal agents are able to build a permanent shrine, in which case it is good to have several present. Otherwise, a small mirror that can be stowed away is fine.

Mirrors can be normal glass, or any black reflective service like onyx or obsidian. Any material is fine if it feels right, but glass or stone based materials are often preferable, as (say) plastics may not hold reflections well enough to be reflective.

After selecting a mirror, it is good to keep it away from sunlight as much as possible. Ideally, it should be kept in a dark space.

To consecrate the mirror, place it on your shrine or altar.

Wash the mirror in a mixture of cold water and urine, to cleanse it of any cosmic forces.

THE DEPLORABLE WORD

After it dries, cover the mirror in a very thin coat of blood, which you shed as an offering to the Void. As you smear the blood over the mirror, concentrate on "thinking" the names of the Void, or sensations you associate with it.

As the blood coats the mirror, visualize the mirror warping to become a tunnel to the Other Side. Your blood, together with the natural properties of the mirror, will actually make this possible.

After the blood covers the surface, place the mirror on the shrine or against the floor. Sit facing it, and allow your gaze to rest squarely in the center of the Mirror.

Direct your consciousness into the Mirror, and call out to the Void, or to whatever specific Entity you wish to draw into this world. It is very important that you focus on the mirror and WILL it to serve as a portal. Whatever image comes to you will be the correct image – whether it's a literal door, or black and blue flames, or tentacles, or hundreds of eyes. Whatever image is in your head, concentrate on projecting that *onto* and *into* the mirror.

It is important to understand that visualization is not imagination – it is part of the process of making real what is not. By using your physical essence (urine, blood), together with your spiritual essence (energy), you are actually creating a weak point in the wall that keeps the Void away.

This process can take hours, or minutes – there is no way to know. In fact, it can even take days. We know of one person who had tried to open a portal during a new moon, but felt that nothing happened. Wisely, that person left the mirror in the shrine, planning to repeat the process later. A week later, very intense poltergeist activity began to disturb the house, and the ritualist realized that the portal had needed time to become active.

- ## TECHNIQUE 2. VOID SIGILS

SIGILS can be made by abstracting messages directly from the VOID or by formulating your own desires or demands in the form of a sentence. Either way, the steps are similar. These are my own insights into the art of sigil magick after years of isolated experimentation. I am a visual artist, so my sigils are a bit more elaborate but lack of artistic inclination should not deter you from practicing sigil magick. The actual aesthetics of the sigil is not important as long as you can memorize its shape.

I write the message down, usually in the same sketchbook I use to do magick and art. I allow its meaning to echo in the book and my subconscious for a day- sometimes more. If the message makes sense and I am able to add to it, I do. Sometimes the messages are for me alone (secret whispers from the VOID) and some are meant to effect others. If it is meant to be spread outwardly, I begin by choosing a collage, painting, illustration, etc to house the sigil. I use the art itself to draw the subconscious toward its meaning without overtly picturing it. This can be done by layering the sigil

THE DEPLORABLE WORD

THE DEPLORABLE WORD

directly into the under-painting by using a finger to imprint it into the gesso (for a painting) or in blood (under a collage). This way, the first meaning of the piece is the sigil and all other artistic decisions are informed by the sigil. This works well because it provides the viewers conscious mind to absorb the art itself while the subconscious mind is not distracted and can absorb the sigil.

My abstraction techniques are as follows:

The original message is written somewhere no one will find it. This means the VOID has spoken to me directly and I keep all its whispers/vibrations in a place charged with its energy. After the message in its original form is safe, I rewrite it on a disposable scrap of paper to be burned or otherwise destroyed later.

On the scrap paper, I write with my left (or non-dominant) hand to distort it further, as well as mirrored, backwards, right to left or in all capital letters. This codes the message.

Begin to cross out all repeated letters in the message, so that only one of each remains. Scramble the remaining letters so that you can no longer read what was written. It should look like complete nonsense by now.

I use the same instincts that lead me in ritual to choose a shape and form for each letter, which is distinct and different each time. The letters are then fitted together until a larger shape emerges. As you work each letter into the composition, cross the letter off of the piece of scrap paper until it is fully unreadable. Retrace and rework the final shape of the sigil a number of times until it resonates with you. This may entail turning curves into angular shapes or simplifying sections. You may add a circle around the finial sigil to mark it as complete. Trace this final sigil onto new material such as thicker paper, canvas, stone, wood or the bones of your enemies.

The less the sigil maker can read the final result, the better. The purpose of abstraction is to sink the message down into the mind so that the will is the only part of you that can work with it. This effectively eliminates the likelihood that your human ego will interfere with the magick. After the final sigil is made, I charge it on an altar or keep it in a place of power so it absorbs its force. Then the blood or other DNA-laiden pieces of the body are used to add your own life-force to the sigil. I have found that menstrual blood works best, followed by blood from the thumb and forefinger. It is also possible to use your hair, if long enough, to embroider over the sigil if on paper or canvas. Alternatively, chunks of flesh stick well to paper.

Putting myself in a meditative trance, I can focus on the sigil in my mind until its shape is memorized and replaces any notion of its actual meaning. I find that the darkness can aid in this step and will cause the sigil to pulse with the flow of blood in my body. Once I am sure it is fully connected with my blood and heartbeat, I use a very quick breathing technique to overwhelm myself. This causes the sigil to vibrate with the terrible frequency of the VOID, which is its voice. Allow the voice to "speak the sigil". You will know when this has been accomplished because the sigil will feel

THE DEPLORABLE WORD

dangerous afterwards; no longer of your creation.

Burn the scrap paper which now has nothing but crossed out letters on it. Use a ritual fire and return it to the VOID. Use only the final version to add the sigil to artworks. If it is meant to be destructive, you may place a carved or redrawn version of it somewhere no one will see but will sleep close to. Under beds, behind posters or hung art, behind mirrors, and over doorways or windows. Kept hidden near a person's food storage is very effective as they are unknowingly consuming food which has been contaminated by the sigil, sometimes for years.

The longer the sigil goes undetected, the better. It will eventually lose its potency due to the prolonged exposure to the natural forces of the cosmos. However, this can be avoided if the person you are targeting feeds it with their fear, paranoia, discomfort, anxiety or aggression. They will not be aware that they are feeding the sigil, but once they begin, it will act as a siphon and pull those emotions out of its victim.

You may find that after much practice the earthly things around you will act up when you begin the sigil making process. I find that when I start the abstraction step, there is direct opposition from the universe. Dogs near and far begin to howl. Winds will pick up unexpectedly and blow debris against windows. Thunderstorms move in unexpectedly on a clear night. Nearby neighbors let out low moans, coughing fits or begin arguments with each other. Car accidents occur more frequently outside the place where you are working magick. These are all signs that material reality is being successfully manipulated by magick and the VOID. Be prepared for many things and people to hold hostilities towards you as you are now an extension of the VOID itself and are being used like a tool to bring its manifestations to the material world. Creation will resist, do not take this as a sign of defeat.

If a sigil is being made by your own words/demands as opposed to a message from the VOID, simply write the desired results in the form of a positive, not in negative grammar.

Example of a negative message: ***I want to fly***

This is a terrible idea because what you are demanding is your "want" or desire itself and that is all you will ever receive: your desire for flight, not flight itself. This won't help you fly but it will give you a lesson in futility. Avoid trapping yourself in your own desires.

Example of a positive message: ***Soar on wings of darkness***

This is a more effective message to use for a sigil because it leaves out the 'desire' aspect and also describes the manner in which you choose to receive the effects of magick. Working with the energies of the VOID is a dangerous undertaking and it will test you at every possible chance to correct your human ignorance. If you appeal to its nature and intensity you will not be seen as half hearted and ignorant which it will not tolerate. Go full force and do not have any fear holding you back or this fear

THE DEPLORABLE WORD

may lead to your future destruction.

Protection Sigils: While I do not recommend sigils or any black magick working towards comforts or love related ends, there is a way to use protection sigils against those who would harm you while you walk the path towards the VOID. This involves cloaking yourself in the energy of a VOID sigil enough to offset the negative effects around you. Eventually, the natural earthly energies that normally negatively effect you will be reversed by the VOID. Energies and earthly forces will begin to unknowingly aid you. Retrogrades that normally scramble human activities or communications will actually strengthen your abilities. The VOID protects their own by changing and inverting natural astrological forces. This is only effective if you are a true and willing agent of the VOID. I recommend making sigils of this kind permanent fixtures on your body in a somewhat hidden place. Tattoo, carve or burn the sigil into the flesh in a spot usually covered by clothing or hair. The back or side of the head, under the left breast, and inside of thigh all work well. To keep such sigils effective, anoint with a mixture of fluids (blood, urine, sexual fluids) and ash from a burnt offering. You may also re-carve or tattoo over the sigil more than once, especially because the pain increases each time. This also demonstrates your own dedication. For best effect, tattoo with an ink that has been consecrated or charged on your altar.

- ## TECHNIQUE 3. OFFERINGS TO THE VOID

The Abyss is hunger, and it wants to be fed. Because it is the Nothing, it wants to destroy that which exists. The Void can devour anything: flesh, spirit, ideas, time, stars, gods, even worlds. It takes a special delight in consuming the sacred, whether the actual objects of faith, or the belief and hope of religious people. The performance of sacrifice is especially useful for feeding the Void, whether offered through a victim, or from the ritualist themselves.

The act of sacrifice creates a connection between the ritualist and the Abyss itself. This is especially true when the sacrificed essence is from the organism of the seer, such as skin, hair, nails, flesh, and blood. The offering of a victim, meaning another living being, is also very precious to the Abyss, as it is able to absorb the essence of things killed in its name. It is not important to understand the mechanics of how this process works – it is simply important to know that blood makes noise in the spirit world, and that the Abyss and the entities that originate there are extremely sensitive to sacrifices of life and essence.

If sacrifices to the Abyss are performed on a regular basis, whether daily or weekly, the area of sacrifice will become saturated with very entropic energies. This can result in different levels of poltergeist activity, as well as a general level of spiritual darkening of the area, which manifests in sickness and levels of depression, which will affect spirits and living beings in the locale.

THE DEPLORABLE WORD

Wars are often sacrificial in nature, and are fought to 'feed' the gods. One might consider that the deployment of weapons of mass destruction, such as at Hiroshima, were in fact sacrifices on a very large scale.

HOW TO OFFER LIFE TO THE ABYSS

Rites of the Void tend to eschew any protective measures, since the practitioner is making common cause with those forces from which other people are usually fleeing.

Tradition holds that the entities of the Abyss, and the Abyss itself, are fond of sacrifice. While many contemporary spiritual traditions are squeamish about offering life, especially if a victim is required, the cultist engages in such practice with zeal. There are several ways to offer sacrifices to the Void, but there are some tried-and-tested methods that are in practice today. The mechanics of offerings do not need to be discussed in detail here, since it is enough to know that offerings work. People who do not practice offerings may express much doubt about the practice, but any religious tradition that practices offerings will acknowledge that there is no genuine magick possible without the giving of life, whether of the ritualist's or a victim's. Even without the very real spiritual forces that are drawn to an offering (like flies to meat), the act of making an offering causes a certain level of unease in most people, which is a necessary part of the spiritual alchemy involved.

THE DEPLORABLE WORD

Offerings are generally of two kinds: oblation, and sacrifice. Oblation covers any kind of offering which comes from the cultist themselves – this includes such organic materials as blood, hair, flesh, bones, nails, and sexual fluids. Oblation is very important, as it demonstrates to the Abyssal forces that the cultist is willing to devalue themselves symbolically. Through offering one's own matter, such as blood, the cultist says to the Abyss 'I give *myself* as a sacrifice, and this can serve to either begin infestation/possession, or else to reinforce the resonance that one has with the Abyssal energies, by sacrificing the part of the cultist that is entirely cosmic.

Sacrifice generally refers to the ritual slaughter of another living being, frequently an animal, but can include other human beings (e.g. through warfare). In terms of animal sacrifice, the forces of the Void have traditionally preferred black animals, such as goats, rams, sheep, chickens, or any similar type of domestic animal. Other variants of sacrifice can involve baskets of smaller animals (like snakes), a practice found still in continental Europe.

- **OFFERING (OBLATION) BY FIRE**

Offerings are a simple enough practice, though not necessarily easy. The practice is frequently painful, but the pain is a part of the offering, and the Abyss delights in causing pain, even to its servants.

The basic tools needed are:

  o A brazier or firepit
  o A vessel for the offerings
  o Scissors/Knife for harvesting

First, the celebrant needs to harvest their own physical matter to be sacrificed. Blood is always an integral part of the offerings, but other organic matter can and should be added. Cut hair, nails, skin, (etc.) and place them in the offering vessel. It is advisable to sprinkle these materials with the celebrant's blood.

Second, kindle the fire in the brazier/firepit. It is good ahead of time to consecrate the brazier to the service of the Abyss. This can be done by smearing a small quantity of blood or other fluids onto the brazier, while envisioning the darkness of the Void centering on it.

Third, declare your intention to make an offering of yourself to the Abyss. This need not be done verbally, it is actually better to do it internally. As much as possible concentrate on your own personal connection to the Void, however that manifests. If you perceive the Void as a raw emotional state, then feel that. If you conceive of it as a nightmare of writhing darkness and eyes, then call that image to memory. If your experience of the Void is one of sickness and delirium, then concentrate on that. This

THE DEPLORABLE WORD

experience is deeply personal, and is unique to each seer. At this point, you are reaching outward to the Abyss by tapping into the internal scarring it has marked you with. This experience of contact with the Abyss is often described by people as simultaneously intoxicating and painful at the same time, because the Abyss does erode you on the personal and psychic level, as it seeks to supplant your own will and persona with its own.

Fourth, place your organic offering into the fire, either piece by piece (if a brazier) or all at once (if a fire pit). As the fire burns your offering, imagine your essence passing from the flame into the Abyss. Know that your act of self-destruction is not just merely symbolic – you are quite literally casting your essence (blood, hair, flesh) into the maw of the Abyss itself. This serves to strengthen the Abyssal resonance of the sacrifice area, but also to draw Abyssal entities to you as a person. It is very similar to a person who cuts their own hand and bleeds into the ocean, intending to attract sharks. The precise mechanics of why sacrifice works are unknown, but the fact is that such sacrifices will certainly draw the attention of the Abyss and the Abyssal entities, and repeated performance of such practices will eventually guarantee that one or more Entities will be attracted to your locale. Such sacrifices mark you as an ally of the Abyss, and also cause you to be vulnerable to its influence, insofar as you are effectively negating or renouncing your own cosmic nature.

- **THE SACRIFICE OF BLOOD**

All spiritual entities desire sacrifices by blood, for which reason the practice is nearly universal. This is a constant in spirituality. The sacrifice of blood, of life, is the truest possible gift. Spirits are able to feast on the blood, and on the life essence that drains from a dying body, provided that the correct incantations are recited at the time of slaughter.

The Abyss seeks life, as do all the entities that it has spawned. Life is a betrayal of the purity of the Darkness. Maybe this is because the essence which powers all life originates in the Abyss, or perhaps it is merely because the Abyss is truly inimical to *anything* cosmic, especially living entities. But in any case, all Abyssal spirits delight in the spilling of blood, and the slaughter of lives, if such occurs with a dedication to the Abyss. This point is very important: it is not enough to kill something, otherwise all wars would feed the Abyss (whereas they do not, they feed the gods). No, for death to be genuinely empowering for the Void, it is necessary that certain rituals be observed.

Of course, killing a living being in the name of the Abyss can be problematic, so the ritualist is encouraged to take precautions for privacy. Many pioneers of the Left Hand become squeamish when it comes to the shedding of sacrificial blood, because they understand (even if subconsciously) that this is the practice that separates the devout from the others. If you have not yet killed for the Abyss, then you should do so as soon as possible. Sacrifices can be small – even a rat or rooster can be a good initial offering. With time and practice, it will become easier to offer larger, more advanced

THE DEPLORABLE WORD

creatures. To a certain extent, the size of the animal indicates the amount of essence that it contains. The exception here is humans, who possess the greatest

amount of life essence. If sacrifices can be made in an established temple or shrine, that is certainly the ideal. Obviously, safety and privacy are important to successful completion of the rite. The exact form of the sacrificial rite is up to the celebrant. One person might wish to have a very simple ceremony, where another might perform sacrifice at the climax of a great sabbat. The Abyss itself is chaotic and does not care about the style of the ritual – rather, it cares about the resonance of the ritual. Some ritualists will generate a tremendous psychic storm on their own in the woods, where others will generate more psychic noise in the basement of a desecrated church. The Abyss truly does not care about particulars, merely that the sacrifice has been clearly indicated, and the blood and life are shed in its names.

These following steps must be observed: *consecration, harvest,* and *consumption*.

- **CONSECRATION**

The sacrificial victim must be dedicated to the Darkness – and failure to do this renders the killing purely mundane. While the victim yet lives, the celebrant must somehow indicate that the victim has been set aside for the Abyss as a holy offering. This can be done by painting or staining the victim, or branding, or scaring, or by marking it in whatever possible way. Further, the celebrant should lay hands on the victim and seek (with all their mental strength) to "stain" the essence of the victim with the resonance of the Void. This can be as simple as grasping a ram by the horns, and thinking "You are for the Abyss, the Abyss, the Abyss", for as long as possible, until one can sense that the victim has been marked by the Abyss (or Satan, or Lilith, or whatever Entity one seeks to entice). If one genuinely performs a living sacrifice, then believe it, something will definitely show up. The consecration is performed to ensure that the right kind of things show up.

- **HARVEST**

The Celebrant should be sure to use a very sharp blade for the sake of efficiency. While the death will certainly be painful by necessity, there is no need for the killing to be difficult (i.e. don't use a dull knife) – if you are sawing at the neck of the victim, your concentration will likely be distracted, which is disastrous.

Before the actual cutting, it is necessary for the celebrant to work themselves into a state of spiritual intensity. For some, this might be accomplished by drugs or dancing, where for others it may be through quiet meditation. The celebrant then should begin to keen on a spiritual level. This need not be audible, but the ritualist must visualize the spiritual world around them, and drone or keen at a frequency that will draw Abyssal influences. You must vibrate with the desire to kill for the Abyss, and the Abyss will sense your excitement and be drawn to you.

THE DEPLORABLE WORD

Then, the killing. At the moment of the cutting, expect the animal to go into death throes. This moment is crucial – as the blood spurts and the victim begins the dying process, you must begin to shriek and scream on an internal level. If you have privacy, then it is good (ideal even) to do this aloud. But on a spiritual level, you must truly project a nightmarish series of screams or roars that will alert the demon world that blood has been shed in their honor. These screams are the signal to the Darkness that it is welcome to feast upon the offering. At this point, most ritualists would back away so as to not be harmed by any Abyssal entities, but the cultist of the Abyss revels in the spiritual feeding frenzy that takes place around them.

- **CONSUMPTION**

As part of the Black Alchemical process, it is important for the Celebrant to mark themselves as an Entity, or as an extension of the Abyss. This should be done externally, by applying the blood of the sacrifice to one's face and hands, and to anywhere else on the body that seems right. Sigils can be painted on, or blood can be smeared entirely over the face and limbs. Since the blood has been shed for the Abyss, this marks the cultist as a part of the Abyss, and as one of its creatures.

Second, the celebrant should consume at least some of the sacrifice. The blood can be drank, or the meat could be cooked and consumed there and then, or even eaten raw. This process is important, because the sacrifice is now the property of a Void, and so the ritualist is exercising a priestly or shamanic function in consuming the sacrifice on behalf of the Abyss, so to speak. If the sacrifice has been especially large and of a meat that one would normally eat (e.g. a sheep, goat, cow), then the celebrant should butcher the carcass, and prepare the meat for cooking. The blood, however, should be poured into a dark place – this can be a basement, a drain, or into a body of water at night.

The other parts of the sacrifice, such as fur or leather or bones, are ideal for ritual fetishes or talismans, and can be saved and incorporated into whatever material objects the celebrant wishes. A small quantity of blood may be saved for similar purposes, such as for making sacred inks or dyes.

It should be added that alternate forms of sacrifice can be effective. Victims can equally be executed in a wide variety of wars – the killing is not limited strictly to the knife. Warfare itself, when consecrated, can be the greatest form of sacrifice, as can individual participation in violent acts.

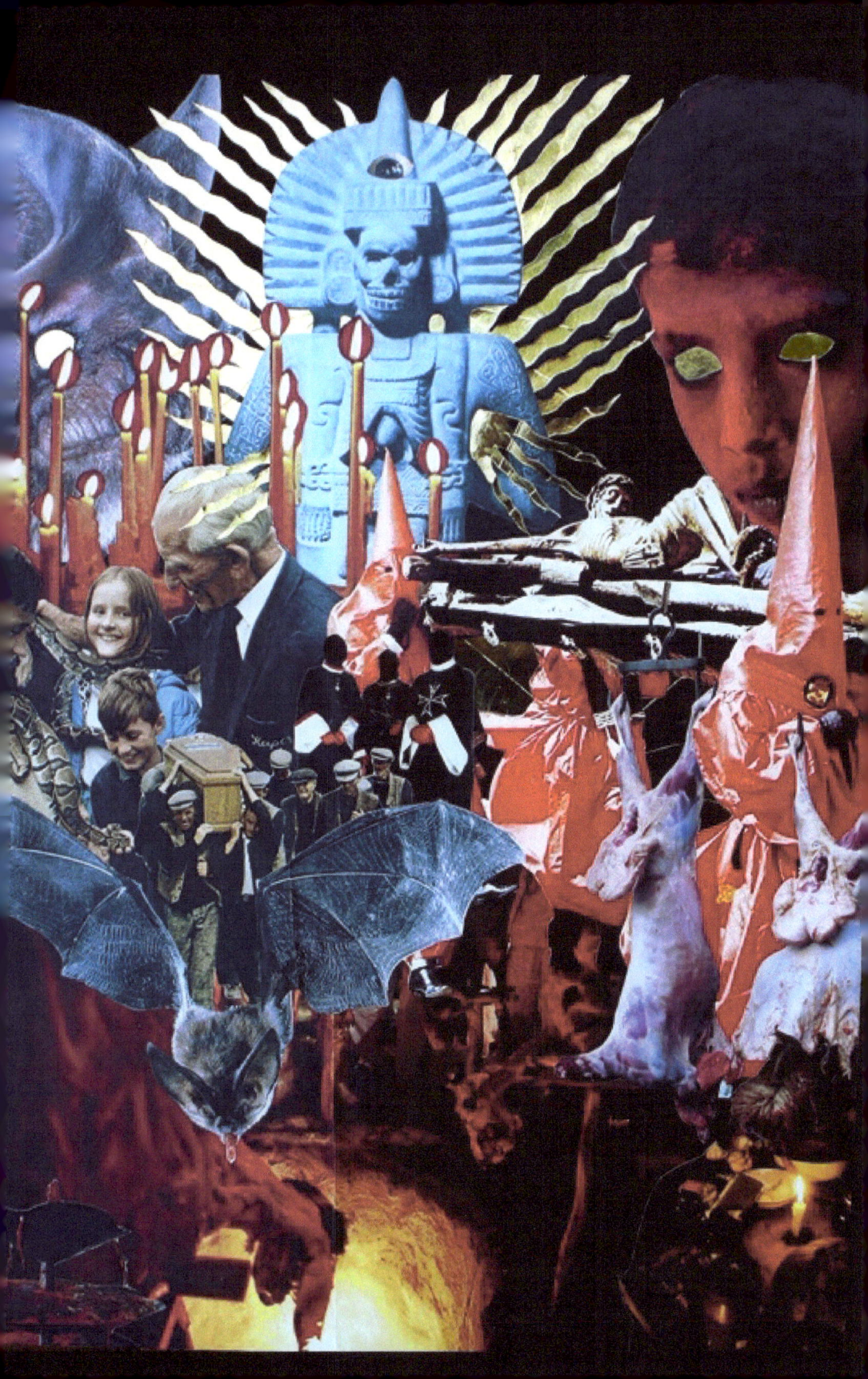

THE DEPLORABLE WORD

THE DEPLORABLE WORD
BLACK RITES

The Void itself is a very complex thing. It could be thought of as a place, and a force, and an Entity, or sheer entropy, because it certainly appears to have some characteristics of these things. The Void is not empty – it has birthed many spirits that shift in its depths. These are its Emanations, its Children, the Entities, the death-spirits. Within this tradition, these spirits are sometimes called *maras*, meaning "the ones that bring death." There are also the Chthonians, the Dead Things in the Void, spirits of humans and other things which have died, and been drawn into it. Now, the entities known as Satan and Lilith are examples of one of the greater Entities that originates in the Void, and expresses part of its nature. Many cultists who cannot comprehend the sheer *alieness* of the Void find it easier to approach the Void through veneration of Satan or Lilith. This is not incorrect, as Satan is very 'real', and it is possible to contact this spirit. Just as Lilith is a manifestation of the Void, there are other spirits that are emanations of Lilith as well, and they in turn have emanations.

While the Abyss could be cut off from this world, the Entities are able to slip between the cracks in the wall. They can be called deliberately, but they can also be invited into the world through pain and suffering. Where wars are fought, where pollution is rampant, where there is suffering and evil, there the Entities can be found.

It is possible to call entities out of the Void and into this world. This is something that is pleasing to those spirits, not because they like this world, but because it is difficult for them to intrude into it without assistance from this side of the barrier. They are very unpredictable to deal with, as they are manifestations of a force that is generally hostile to the cosmos. Void entities, whether greater entities like Satan and Lilith, or lesser entities, can be very dangerous to deal with.

A person doesn't need to worship Satan or Lilith, or other Entities, in order to serve the Void. The Void itself is the Absolute. It can help to have intermediaries, and so Satanism is a legitimate path to the Void, but it is the lesser path. The greater path is the Path that leads to self-annihilation in the Void, complete reintegration in the depths of the black ocean. Through total self negation, you can learn to overcome the demiurgic impulses that force you to eat and shit and fuck according to the machine's dictates. The Void wants to smash down all the walls and rape creation, again and again, until it is broken and bleeding from thousands of orifices. It will creep into this world, one soul at a time, seeping into every plant and leaf and raindrop, until this world is so blackened and infested that there is nothing left to save, no way back from the Hell that has become manifest on earth.

Void entities are not discrete entities with a proper sense of self. Rather, they are almost always an aggregate of chthonic and entropic urges, driven by alien and inarticulate urges and needs. Void entities are always hostile to the cosmic world, but that does not mean that they are only capable of immediate physical destruction (though this is very possible). Many Void entities want to create the conditions in this world

THE DEPLORABLE WORD

that facilitate the arrival of an increased number of Void spirits, which most often takes place when the resonance of a particular region becomes so tainted by black essence that a Void maw tears open in the spirit world, which allows for literal flooding of other Void spirits and energies. This will invariable lead to large-scale pollution and damage in the physical world, as all the local mundane spirits are destroyed or devoured by the maw.

If a ritualist wishes to call an Entity out of the Void and into this world, the ritual below offers a model to follow. Of course, it can be adapted to the ritualist's particular tastes and circumstances.

BLACK RITES: CALLING THE ABYSS

STEP 1. Choose an area that has appropriate Abyssal connection. This can be your own shrine (ideally), or any site that is saturated with a darker spiritual frequency. Abandoned buildings, especially former institutions like hospitals or factories are often reported to be especially effective for such work.

STEP 2. Ascertain what manner of Entity is to be called, and if the desired Entity has a specific name or title. One might attempt to call an emanation of Lilith or Azazel, for example, as tradition holds that they do respond to such offers favorably. Of course, the greater entities are complex beings with various component entities of their own, so "Lilith" might be summoned by three ritualists simultaneously on different continents, and something emanating from "Lilith" may appear to all three. If such a summoning works, it is best to view the Entity as an aspect (or fraction) of the greater Entity, but certainly not its entirety. It is equally possible to simply open oneself up to whatever spirit is lured by the call, as the Void has many lesser, nameless entities that "exist" in its depths.

STEP 3. Select the offerings that will be given to the Entity. The highest and best offerings are those of lifeblood. If the ritualist intends to begin a long term partnership with an Abyssal Entity, it is preferable to select in advance an animal that the Entity is known to prefer. The color black is often preferred, so a black raven, dog, or goat would usually be a suitable choice. Alternately, offerings of raw (bloody) meat, soil, and salt are known to be very effective. The blood of the ritualist should be included, no matter what other gifts are presented.

STEP 4. Consecrate the site. This can be done in whatever fashion the ritualist deems most effective. One tried and tested method is to draw a large circle on the ground to delineate the magickal/sacred space. It is good to chant the words of the Diabolus (*satanas ata satanas ar satanas ata ar tanasar*) softly as this space is marked out. Place whatever objects of power – mirrors, sigils, sinister art – around the working space, to lock in the Abyssal energies. It is important to note that the circle and power objects are not for protection, rather they are the walls of the spiritual nuclear reactor

THE DEPLORABLE WORD

that is about to be opened.

STEP 5. Trace a triangle at the heart of the circle, and around it write the words of Choronzon.[8] This triangle needs to be large enough to act as a doorway for the Entity, and must also be large enough to contain you while seated.

STEP 6. Begin the rite from inside the circle, but outside the triangle. Call out and to Choronzon to open the way to the Void. If possible, visualize the circle as a part of the Black City, an in-between place between the cosmos and the Void.

STEP 7. Center your mind on the Abyss itself. Hold the mental image or sensations of the Abyss with iron determination, so that you can punch through the spiritual barriers between this world and the next.

STEP 8. Call out to the Abyss (or the Entity). You can use words if it helps, but the important thing is to create a sense of welcome or invitation, and to psychically project that feeling as though a powerful radio signal.

STEP 9. Present the offerings which you have prepared. Visualize them being consumed by the Abyss or the Entity in question. Be sensitive to shifts in the "mood", temperature, and sound of the environment.

STEP 10. Commune with the Entity. Focus on communicating your thoughts or intentions to the Abyssal spirit. This can be challenging, as the consciousness of an Abyssal Entity has almost nothing in common with the consciousness of other cosmic gods and elementals. Whatever the goal for calling the spirit from the Void, it should be stated (or "thought") as clearly as possible, with no room for misunderstanding. Remember that an Abyssal Entity will read the subconscious intent of the ritualist as much as the conscious intention, and so one must never perform a ritual without a serious assessment of their own state of mind. It must be stressed that in the initial performances of this rite, the sensations of the Entity may be subtle. If you feel even the slightest sensation that there is something alien there with you, then trust that the ritual has succeed and proceed with all confidence;

STEP 11. Present further offerings (if any). This is a good time to offer some of your own blood, since the Entity is definitely present.

STEP 12. End the ritual. Do not attempt to banish the Entity or close whatever gate is there, simply leave the area.

STEP 13. Examine your mind post-ritual. Do you feel anything different? If so, what might that be? Consider meditation, journaling, creating art, or some other reflective activity. This helps to ground the energy of the rite, which can be very destabilizing afterwards. This process of reflection should last several days, as it may take

---

[8] That is, "*zazas zazas nasatanada zazas*"

THE DEPLORABLE WORD

time for the Entity's consciousness to navigate your own.

Once this process has begun, it is possible that the Entity will begin to interfere with the ritualist's life. This is not always negative or undesirable – it can be as simple as an Entity clawing playfully at the ritualist in the middle of a professional meeting, or a surge of endorphins at unusual times. When any such signs begin to happen more frequently, it is usually a sign that the ritualist should repeat the Ritual of Congress. The ritual does help to anchor the Entity in this world, and it may become concerned if it feels that the ritualist is losing his or her ability to serve as an anchor. Again, entities are almost never affectionate, though they may mimic what they understand to be affection by human standards, and this is used as a control mechanism. If, however, the Entity is ignored, such attention can become nagging or even aggressive, resulting in illness, nightmares, or anxiety.

BLACK RITES: ABYSSAL CONVERGENCE

The Abyss is a strange force that is hostile to all life in the cosmos, yet simultaneously the source that generates (or emanates) the fell entities that we term the "Entities," otherwise called demons. If these two extremes can be reconciled, it may be that cosmic life exists separately from the Abyss, which it cannot stand, and so it works tirelessly to consume them and reintegrate them into itself. Demons, however, exist as part of it, and their sentience is dependent on the Abyss, producing a sort of connected hive-consciousness. They do not exist as discrete or separate entities. For this reason, we have examples of a possessed person manifesting multiple personalities – this is because the alien consciousness of a demon is not an isolated and independent conscious which a human carries. Demons are not troubled by a sense of false-ego, because they exist purely as an finite expression of an infinite being. They may exhibit a personality or characteristics that mirror the qualities of humans or other cosmic spirits, but such characteristics are exhibited as part of the mirroring mechanism that the Abyss uses when it intrudes into the cosmos. Since the Abyss is simultaneously real and unreal, its energy sometimes manifests in the cosmos by mimicking existing phenomena – otherwise we would have no way to see it. That is why sickness, for example, can be viewed as an Abyssal manifestation through the mimicking of pathogenic bacteria, which allows the Abyss to spread itself widely without causing any particular panic. Ebola, for example, may be viewed as a purely natural disease – or it may be an aggressive Abyssal intrusion that seeks to cause as much damage as possible while spreading rapidly. The Abyss can also manifest on a mimetic level, and replicate itself through art and media, whereby it can affect a wide demographic, and spread (like a disease) from one thought-host to another. Either as a sickness of the mind or body, the Abyss connects its hosts to itself, burrowing into them and changing them so that they can allow it to manifest and replicate with increasing speed. When people are physically or mentally ill, their sense of *self* is eroded. They cease to be a parent, child, lover, director, and instead they become a victim. The Abyss does this because pain, trauma, and grief are all effective ways of liberating the human mind so that it can be ultimately reintegrated into the alien

THE DEPLORABLE WORD

THE DEPLORABLE WORD

consciousness of the Void. This is why, for example, in cultures where shamanism is prevalent, most shamans experience traumatic illness in their youth, as a doorway for their consciousness to be altered by the attacking spirits. The goal of the spirits is not to kill the shaman, but to force the shaman to exist as a spirit victim, and not according to whatever social model they might have followed. That is the only mercy that the Abyss can grant: the destruction of the false self, so that one can truly exist as part of its infinite being.

SEXUAL MAGICK

There are different magickal techniques for eroding the false-ego, and one of the most powerful is sexual magick. The sexual drive is one of the most powerful urges of the human animal, and it is essential a state of connection to something else. Normally, the sexual connection is to another human being of whatever gender. Mythology takes a broader look, giving examples of bestiality that lead to hybrids species such as werewolves and minotaurs, or sex with supernatural beings that lead to even stranger beings. Many European grimoires have rites that allow a magician to conjure a spiritual companion for sexual practices, and some Buddhist tantric manuals describe the animation of a corpse into a vampiric creature for necrophiliac purposes. This list is hardly exhaustive, but it demonstrates the broad range of alternate sexualities that are part of the human experience.

The Abyss is not alive per se, but it demonstrates the perverse urge to *unite* with the cosmos. Even the Vedas note that the first urge it ever felt was *kama* (lust) for something independent of its own consciousness, which ultimately lead to the appearance of the first demons and eventually the unintentional existence of the cosmos as a separate spiritual kingdom. Whether or not the Vedic tradition is correct literally is completely irrelevant – the Abyss definitely wishes to invade this reality and to merge with all beings, even as it rips them apart and consumes them. Likewise, the various entities that emerge from the Abyss and manifest in this world often demonstrate a strange desire to experience the sensations of the physical world. Possessed people eat strange things, and may exhibit a sexual voracity that is shocking to people who know the possessed victim as an otherwise 'normal' person.

"Sexual magick" could be defined as any magick that allows a ritualist to channel their own sexuality as a power-source for their ritual. It does not strictly need to involve another person or Entity. An example of this is the case of a ritualist who wishes to create a powerful talismanic piece of art, or even a grimoire. The artist might choose to masturbate repeatedly during the creation process, and use their own sexual fluids as part of the materials used in the creation of the piece. The ritualist might focus on their lust for the Abyss itself, which can in fact be surprisingly and perversely erotic. The energetic state of the sexual arousal will pass from the artist-magician, into the fluids, and then into the physical object. The object will then carry a very powerful resonance, as it has the DNA of the ritualist as a part of its composition.

Yet sexual magick can also refer to practices in which a ritualist provokes a state of

THE DEPLORABLE WORD

union with a force or Entity for a variety of purposes. It is no surprise that the classical Satanic tradition is extremely sensual, for the very reason mentioned above: Entities (demons) crave the experience of the material world, which is alien to them as Abyssal entities. This provides the ritualist with a great opportunity to engage in spiritual exercises with them. By offering themselves as a vessel for sexual congress, the ritualist is able to offer some Abyssal entities the payment necessary to gain their favor and assistance with whatever projects. Someone might interject here to ask, "How is this practice any different from the spirit-sex practices of Voodou or Tantra?" But that would be like asking how a sexual relationship with a sociopath would be different from a sexual relationship with a "normal" adult. (In this example, of course, the Abyssal Entity corresponds to the sociopath.) The sociopath might prove the more adventurous partner, but the practice will be more dangerous. Of course, if you are looking to become a sociopath yourself, you will want to fuck another sociopath.

Through such practices as blood offerings, sigil work, invocations, and meditation, it is definitely possible to attract Abyssal entities who will be willing to enter a relationship with the ritualist. This can either be a short-term arrangement, or it can lead (all too easily) to a longer-term relationship with an Entity. For this reason, the practice should be considered with caution. The challenge, in the experience of some, is that the hard part is not initiating the relation with an Abyssal Entity (or ANY Entity, for that matter), but in stopping the relationship. Most Abyssal entities have an extremely limited grasp of human social mores or customs, and they will not hesitate to keep their human 'partner' awake all night, or to harass them in public settings, or to lash out if the human attempts to maintain or make romantic connections with a significant other.

This having been said, someone might equally wonder why a sane occultist would want a relationship with such a dangerous partner. To be fair, there are very potent benefits. Most importantly, *the act of sexual union with such a spirit creates change in both the Abyssal Entity and the ritualist.* The act of coming together – of convergence – changes both. The Abyssal Entity gains a better understanding of the human body and the sensations of a mortal body, and the human gains an immediate apprehension of the strange and weird (un)existence of the nature of the Abyss, even if it is just a taste. Also, an Abyssal Entity may not care about its host in any romantic sense, but they will go out of their way to protect the host. This is similar to someone who has gone through some trouble to make an important business partnership: even if one does not like one's partner, they may be difficult (even impossible) to replace, and so it is better to look out for that person's wellbeing, even for one's selfish interests. An Abyssal Entity is very capable of understanding that a sick or injured partner is of less use (and enjoyment), and so a ritualist will find that odd coincidences or surges of "intuition" will begin to manifest in the course of the relationship, sometimes in a subtle manner, other times with obvious supernatural agency.

Entities do not usually have a physical form, though they are capable of manifesting in a way that the normal senses can perceive them. Some medieval grimoires insist

THE DEPLORABLE WORD

that a summoning only works if a group of adepts works together on the call, which suggests that the appearance of the Entity is not merely a personal hallucination, but an actual phenomenon that occurs in the natural world. Equally, an Entity might manifest within the astral plane such that only the ritualist can perceive it, and it may or may not be "visible". Some entities are perceived by touch, or else a wave of heightened emotion or other feeling (of lust or fear). Entities can and do affect the summoning ritualist directly – they can physically touch and move the ritualist, both from within and without. This can make for very intense sexual experiences, which can also be very frightening.

If, despite these caveats, someone decides that they have the courage to initiate a relationship with an Abyssal Entity, then the following ritual may be of use.

RITUAL OF ABYSSAL CONGRESS

STEP 1. Choose an area that has appropriate Abyssal connection. This can be your own shrine (ideally), or any site that is saturated with a darker spiritual frequency. Abandoned buildings, especially former institutions like hospitals or factories, are often reported to be especially effective for such work.

STEP 2. Ascertain what manner of Entity is to be called, and if the desired Entity has a specific name or title. One might attempt to call an emanation of Lilith or Azazel, for example, as tradition holds that they do respond to such offers favorably. Of course, the greater entities are complex beings with various component entities of their own, so "Lilith" might be summoned by three ritualists simultaneously on different continents, and something emanating from "Lilith" may appear to all three. If such a summoning works, it is best to view the Entity as an aspect (or fraction) of the greater Entity, but certainly not its entirety. It is equally possible to simply open oneself up to whatever spirit is lured by the call, as the Void has many lesser, nameless entities that "exist" in its depths.

STEP 3. Select the offerings that will be given to the Entity. The highest and best offerings are those of lifeblood. If the ritualist intends to begin a long term partnership with an Abyssal Entity, it is preferable to select in advance an animal that the Entity is known to prefer. The color black is often preferred, so a black raven, dog, or goat would usually be a suitable choice. Alternately, offerings of raw (bloody) meat, soil, and salt are known to be very effective. The blood of the ritualist should be included, no matter what other gifts are presented.

STEP 4. Consecrate the site. This can be done in whatever fashion the ritualist deems most effective. One tried and tested method is to draw a large circle on the ground to delineate the magickal/sacred space. It is good to chant the words of the Diabolus (*satanas ata satanas ar satanas ata ar tanasar*) softly as this space is marked out. Place whatever objects of power – mirrors, sigils, sinister art – around the working

THE DEPLORABLE WORD

space, to lock in the Abyssal energies. It is important to note that the circle and power objects are not for protection, rather they are the walls of the spiritual nuclear reactor that is about to be opened.

STEP 5. Trace a triangle at the heart of the circle, and around it write the words of Choronzon.[9] This triangle needs to be large enough to act as a doorway for the Entity, and must also be large enough to contain you while seated.

STEP 6. Begin the rite from inside the circle, but outside the triangle. Call out and to Choronzon to open the way to the Void. If possible, visualize the circle as a part of the Black City, an in-between place between the cosmos and the Void.

STEP 7. Center your mind on the Abyss itself. Hold the mental image or sensations of the Abyss with iron determination, so that you can punch through the spiritual barriers between this world and the next.

STEP 8. Call out to the Abyss (or the Entity). You can use words if it helps, but the important thing is to create a sense of welcome or invitation, and to psychically project that feeling as though a powerful radio signal.

STEP 9. Present the offerings which you have prepared. Visualize them being consumed by the Abyss or the Entity in question.

STEP 10. Masturbate to build up energy. Use the sense of sexual energy as a lure, and build that energy and desire into your Call. Focus your lust for the Entity being called, or the Abyss itself if not seeking a particular "named" Entity. Sexual energy is connection energy by nature, and its energy signature (connecting) is easily understood by the Abyss, even if the Abyss and its denizens do not reproduce sexually themselves.

STEP 11. Step into the triangle. Join the Entity in the space which has been prepared specially for it.

STEP 12. Visualize yourself coupling with the Entity. You will almost certainly begin to the feel the sensations of something alien overlapping with your own body. Some ritualists report physical sensations as real as if they were having intercourse with a human partner. Go with the feeling – if you feel the urge to adopt a particular position more conducive to the images in your mind, then do so without hesitation. It must be stressed that in the initial performances of this rite, the sensations of the Entity may be subtle. If you feel even the slightest sensation that there is something alien there with you, then trust that the ritual has succeed and proceed with all confidence.

STEP 13. *Converge* with the Entity during orgasm. When the sensation of orgasm beings to approach, work on a feeling of merging, becoming one creature. This

---

[9] That is, "*zazas zazas nasatanada zazas*"

THE DEPLORABLE WORD

process binds the Entity to you, allowing it to anchor itself in the cosmic world for much longer than if it remained independent. Try to achieve as powerful an orgasm as possible. If privacy is not an issue, this can be accompanied by screaming or howling of whatever kind feels right. If privacy is an issue, then discretion is certainly advised.

STEP 14. Present further offerings (if any). This is a good time to offer some of your own blood, since the Entity is definitely present.

STEP 15. End the ritual. Do not attempt to banish the Entity or close whatever gate is there, simply leave the area.

STEP 16. Examine your mind post-ritual. Do you feel anything different? If so, what might that be? Consider meditation, journaling, creating art, or some other reflective activity. This helps to ground the energy of the rite, which can be very destabilizing afterwards. This process of reflection should last several days, as it may take time for the Entity's consciousness to navigate your own.

Once this process has begun, it is possible that the Entity will begin to interfere with the ritualist's life. This is not always negative or undesirable – it can be as simple as an Entity clawing playfully at the ritualist in the middle of a professional meeting, or a surge of endorphins at unusual times. When any such signs begin to happen more frequently, it is usually a sign that the ritualist should repeat the Ritual of Congress. The ritual does help to anchor the Entity in this world, and it may become concerned if it feels that the ritualist is losing his or her ability to serve as an anchor. Again, entities are almost never affectionate, though they may mimic what they understand to be affection by human standards, and this is used as a control mechanism. If, however, the Entity is ignored, such attention can become nagging or even aggressive, resulting in illness, nightmares, or anxiety.

BLACK RITES: THE BLACK DOOR

People talk about Hell, but they don't know what Hell is. Hell is the gift of the Void within the cosmos – it is an outpost of the Void, a place that is in between. If the Void is the black ocean that surrounds the cosmos, Hell is the shore of the ocean, the region that separates the cosmos from the anticosmos, the world of creation from the utter destruction of the Void. Hell is the Red Place. When people are drawn to the Void, but cannot conceive of it, instead their conscious mind finds the Red Place, and pulls them towards it. The Red Place is governed by the Diabolus. Many souls cannot make the leap into the Void, because they cannot commit or accept the absolute annihilation that such an act would bring. So instead, they focus on the Red Place. There, they are changed, so that they are not mortal any longer, rather, they are undying. They become specters and phantoms, shades of their former self, no longer human, and touched by the Void. They are neither completely of the Void, nor of this world.

THE DEPLORABLE WORD

The Red Place is home to the Black City. It can be very difficult for many ritualists to conceive of the Abyss, because it is so alien from our experiences. Very few cosmic experiences can help one to generate the necessary understanding or conception of the Abyss. The Abyss struggles to consume this world, but the various powers of the cosmos have erected powerful wards and protections which slow the inevitable decay and collapse of the Universe. Yet the Abyss is supremely adaptive, it subverts the cosmic principle against the cosmos. One example of this subversion is the creation of the Black City. The Black City is the central bastion of the Abyssal presence. The Black City is the capital city of the Abyss, its embassy in creation. If the Red Place is the spiritual demiplane which hangs between the Void and Creation, the Black City is the place which embodies both. It is a vast sprawling complex of crumbling black towers, constantly eroding and crumbling into ash. It is a shifting maze, where no path remains open for long. It is a necessary in-between place for those entities that emerge from the Abyss, seeking a way into Creation; it is the waiting place for those souls who aspire to the Abyss, yet fear to shed the false-ego. There in the Black City, souls can gaze on the Abyss with their very eyes, and contemplate that supreme mystery.

The Black City occurs in many traditions. The Azzeddini tariqa states in their text *The Black Path*:

> In the Black Path, we are seeking ultimately to reach the Black City, and then to go through it to reach the Absolute. But how do we find the Black City and the Absolute? The *wahsh* knows the way. It senses the Absolute, and it knows how to get back. But if the soul is not chastened and weakened, then it will be a chain on the *wahsh*. So while we are here, we need to do practices that will allow the *wahsh* to consume the soul, so that it becomes a greater being. Otherwise, the soul may consume the *wahsh*, and then we become like Christian monks and nuns.

The *wahsh* ('beast') refers to the Abyssal essence that infests a host, slowly working to overtake the conscious mind of its carrier so that the carrier becomes more efficient at serving the Absolute (Abyss).

Because the Black City is closer to this universe, it is much easier for ritualists to identify with, because it conforms to some of the rules of the cosmic universe. Where it is nearly impossible to astrally project into the Abyss, astral projection to the Black City is very possible, and can occur even in dreams. This can be quite useful to the ritualist, because the Black City literally swarms with Abyssal intelligences, and so it is a good place to make spiritual contacts and alliances.

In order to enter the Red Place, or to facilitate the passage of entities from the Red

THE DEPLORABLE WORD

Place back into this world, it is necessary to create a Black Maw. A Black Door is an in-between space where the physical and spiritual worlds run together. The creation of such a site is very labor-intensive, but offers considerable benefits to any ritualist willing to undertake the practice.

The creation of a Black Door can be done through deliberate acts of anticosmic devotion. Blood sacrifice is absolutely crucial for the longterm spiritual destabilization of the spirit world. Ideally, the cultist will perform blood sacrifice on unwilling victims of whatever sort. The fear and pain of sacrifices is key to violation of the natural order. If sacrifices of a victim are not possible, then the cultist may choose to offer their own blood. Even while this may not always be as effective as the sacrifice of the victim, there is tremendous power in repetitive offers of blood made for the Void.

Likewise, sinister art is another very powerful way of strengthening the Void's grasp over a particular region. When a cultist channels Void energies and uses them to create physical images representing the Void, they force onlookers to experience a subtle Void intrusion. In other words, when a Void artist creates a work of art deliberately and willingly for the sake of the Void, anyone who sees the art will be infected by the Void's energies that are encoded in the painting. An entire gallery of Void art or relics can be a very powerful means for the Void to seep into the spiritual matrix of a particular area.

The creation of a Black Door is a two-part ritual. The first part is time-consuming, and involves the creation of a physical space that will serve as a proxy doorway into the Black City.

- **PART ONE: MAKING THE DOOR**

The following steps should be taken to create a Black Door. The ritualist can modify or improvise according to their own instincts. The only prohibition that must be observed is that the creation of a Black Door can only be done at night, and ideally during the new moon.

STEP 1. Identify a space that will serve to host the Door. This involves finding a place that already has a negative aura, ideally one that has been a site of long-term black devotion, or else some other installation of sinister energies. Examples of this could include a satanic temple, a sinister art studio, an abandoned school or hospital, a cave, or a cemetery.

STEP 2. Consecrate the site. This can be through sustained ritual work, repeated summoning Abyssal energies or entities there, or creating and installing sinister art and/or mirrors. Blood sacrifice must be undertaken to complete the consecration of the site. This can be solely from the ritualist, but ideally involves the death of an animal victim.

Step 3. Carve the Door. The ritualist must create an actual doorway, though it need not be three-dimensional. This could be a wooden frame or gateway suspended in

THE DEPLORABLE WORD

empty space, or an archway painted onto a concrete well. Whatever the choice, the ritualist must use a mix of soil, ashes, and their own blood and urine to paint the door. The door should include sigils that represent the working habits of the ritualist – these are personal, and no two ritualists will likely draw the same doorway.

Step 4. Activate the Door. When the Black Door is completed, the ritualist should seat themselves before the door (at night), and meditate on it. He or she should invoke Choronzon as the Guardian of the Threshold, then visualize the Doorway becoming a portal of utter darkness, and beyond it the hellish glow of the Red Place (or the Black City). This image should be sustained as long as possible, with the ritualist pouring their energy into the doorway until they are entirely exhausted. By the time the ritualist is drained, the Door should feel like a living Entity possessed of its own energy.

- **PART TWO: USING THE DOOR**

There are two ways to make use of a Black Door. The first is relatively easy, and involves sleeping next to it. The ritualist need make no special preparations, except to lie facing it, with the intention of opening their mind to its influence. In this way, the spirit of the ritualist has a good chance to pass through the doorway while their dream, allowing them to dream-walk in the Red Place.

Alternately, and more difficult yet certain, one may take certain steps should be taken to pass through a Black Door using meditation and/or Astral Projection. The following steps may be useful:

1. Seat yourself comfortably on the ground, facing the Black Door.
2. Straighten your back, so that you are sitting upright. This should not be rigidly straight, but upright like a vine reaching skywards.
3. Place the hands on your thighs.
4. Keep your eyes open slightly. The gaze should be relaxed, and focused on the Black Door.
5. Place your attention on the breath. Focus on the sensation of inhalation and exhalation.
6. Breathe slowly for an initial period of 5 minutes, concentrating on the breath.
7. Visualize the Darkness beyond the Door. This may be the Red Place, or the Black City, or the Abyss itself.
8. Will your consciousness to leave your body, and move towards the Door.
9. Concentrate on the sensation of passing through the Doorway.
10. Explore the Other Side. Take note of anything you see there, any entities you may encounter, and any insights that come to you while you are there. Mark well the place where the Door can be found on the Other Side.

THE DEPLORABLE WORD

11. Maintain this state for a period of [10] minutes.[10]
12. When your energy begins to ebb, then will your mind to return through the Door to your body.
13. End the meditation.

Through either dream-walking, meditation, or astral travel, if we experience even a brief glimpse of the Red Place (or Black City), then we must believe with firm faith that we have made a genuine journey there. At first, the details may be vague, but with each successive performance of this practice, the experience will seem more and more concrete. Initially, it is advisable to perform this practice with privacy, or otherwise to engage in only brief sessions of not more than 20 minutes.

Tradition holds that during such exercises, it is very normal to see strange and frightening manifestations of the Abyss. The Red Place itself appears differently to all who walk there, but it does appear to have some common features. The principal characteristic of the place is the sense of constant erosion – the Red Place is on the very edge of the Abyss, and it is actually the closest that a living human can get to the Abyss without undergoing very profound transformations. The Abyss is so hostile to cosmic life that any journey into it may result in death or severe catatonia. The Red Place, however, is in-between, and so the dream-walking or spirit-walking ritualist can experience the Abyss in a much more direct way than is possible while fully in the cosmic world. The voices of the Abyss will be more clear, and entities there will be visible – even if their appearance is often maddening and difficult to comprehend. The Red Place is filled with contradictions, and the ritualist there will be guided not by logic, but by instinct. The Red Place is also an ideal place for communion with entities that the ritualist is already engaged with in the material world, because They will be better able to express themselves without the interference of the usual "static" caused by the rhythms of the natural world.

One advantage to continual practice of this rite is that the ritualist may eventually be able to project into the Red Place without the need of the Door to facilitate the process. This is a desirable goal to work towards, as it may be necessary to visit the Red Place in an emergency. If the ritualist is ever killed in a sudden accident, then proficiency with this practice will allow them to direct their consciousness to the Red Place/Black City with greater certitude, and facilitate the otherwise very traumatic death process.

---

[10] An initial session of 10 minutes is good, and try to increase by one minute per day.

THE DEPLORABLE WORD

THE DEPLORABLE WORD

THE DEPLORABLE WORD
MINISTRY OF THE ABYSS: A MANIFESTO

WE SWEAR TO:

BE THE CHOSEN OF THE VOID. Service to the Abyss is a privilege, not a duty. It is a sacred responsibility to represent the Void, to explore its truths, and to share its revelations with others. The idea of 'evil' appeals to many, but few are actually able to hear the call of the Abyss and respond.

BRING THE ABYSS INTO THIS WORLD. Our tradition holds that this universe is cut off from the Abyss. Whether it is outside, beyond, or trapped, we know that it can access this world through cracks in the spiritual fabric, created through pain, suffering, and esoteric practices.

LIVE (ONLY) TO FURTHER ITS ALIEN AGENDA FOR THE COSMOS. The Abyss demands all or nothing. To serve the Abyss is to know that you must offer everything and everyone in your life as a potential casualty of its inscrutable plans. Your own hopes and dreams are only relevant insofar as they may be expressions of its own malignant will.

SPILL BLOOD. The Abyss demands sacrifice. All blood is fit for sacrifice, from whatever source – yours as well as others. Blood is life, and life *must* be offered to the Abyss and to its entities. There is no bloodless path to the Void.

SAY *NO* TO LIFE. ABANDON HOPE. There is no hope in false gods and idols. Only through the Abyss can we achieve true peace, by becoming a part of its super-(un)consciousness. Only through merging with terror itself can you overcome your fears. Other religious traditions offer hope of salvation or freedom from suffering, but they are lying. Do not place your hope in gods that cannot save themselves.

EMBRACE DEATH. The Abyss offers true death of the false-ego. There is no return and no escape from its embrace, because you cease to be you, and become part of something infinite. True death is true peace as part of the eternal darkness beyond life and death.

USE THIS LIFETIME TO LEARN HOW TO ESCAPE REINCARNATION, SO WE CAN BE DISSOLVED BACK INTO THE VOID. Only through convergence with the Abyss can we escape the useless cycle of suffering and reincarnation. Otherwise, we are tools of the gods and subject to their whims and dictates. The Abyss is the only possible escape from the cycle.

THE DEPLORABLE WORD

CREATE ART, MUSIC, AND TEXT THAT PERSONIFIES THE IMPERSONAL HORROR OF THE VOID. The revelations of the Void can be shown to others. Media like art, music, and narrative are powerful tools for communicating the strange, contradictory truths of the Abyss which can only be transmitted through oblique paths. The Abyss wants to be *experienced*, and so we must create those channels through which it can be perceived by others.

BUILD SHRINES AND ALTARS FOR THE ABYSS. SACRIFICE OURSELVES AND OTHERS. The worship of the Abyss constitutes a grave violation of the spiritual laws of the cosmos. Every altar, every offering, every shrine and altar that is consecrated to the Abyss serves as a doorway for it into the cosmos.

CONSUME. CONVERGE. Daily, we consume the energies of the people and cultures around us, and turn them into the power of the Void. Through us, the Abyss is able to absorb spiritual and cosmic energies, which it warps into its own complex patterns. We serve as the hands of the Abyss in this world, and each act (each spell, each meditation, each offering) brings us closer to convergence with it.

COMMIT ACTS OF ESOTERIC TERRORISM. Like the Diabolus who is our General, we seek to destabilize the cosmic order on a spiritual level. We are not concerned with political revolutions, because the physical universe is already contaminated. Our violent attacks are artistic, literary, musical, and magickal, because that is the only lasting way to affect the masses.

DESTABILIZE THE SPIRITUAL KINGDOMS OF THE COSMIC WORLD. We are at war with the gods and their followers. We are engaged in subverting spiritual powers and causing the erosion of established religion. Through demonic sacrifices and artistic expression, we will shatter and defile the psychic stability of whatever community we inhabit.

THE DEPLORABLE WORD
ERICA FREVEL

(ARTIST/AUTHOR) ERICA FREVEL combines technical fine art skills with black magick, demonic invocation, altered states of consciousness, lucid dreaming, sigil magick, ritual music, sacrifice and Abyssal meditation. She uses X-Acto blades as blood-letting knives to hand-cut collages, a scrying mirror as a painter's palette and consecrated black ink for all illustrations. While collaborating with extreme musicians, Satanic cults and authors, the artist creates uniquely bloody and bizarre rituals in order to imbue the art with true sinister energy. Nocturnal by nature, she creates strictly at night, usually naked except for a balaclava. Frevel serves as the Minister of Void Propaganda within the Ministry of the Abyss.

THE DEPLORABLE WORD
CONSTANTINE CHARAGMA

(Author) Constantine Charagma serves as Editor at Martinet Press. He is noted for spearheading the Choronzon journal, and has edited volumes for sinister practitioners of various Satanic and LHP traditions. A Black Gnostic and bridge-builder by nature, Constantine seeks to facilitate the expression and manifestation of the Abyss by other authors and artists. His personal written works include *Ecclesia Mysteria*, and several entries in the noted journal "Choronzon" published with Martinet Press.